*Two Early Renaissance Bird Poems*

# TWO EARLY RENAISSANCE BIRD POEMS

## The Harmony of Birds

## The Parliament of Birds

Edited,
with Introduction and Notes by
MALCOLM ANDREW

THE RENAISSANCE ENGLISH TEXT SOCIETY
AND THE NEWBERRY LIBRARY

FOLGER BOOKS
WASHINGTON: THE FOLGER SHAKESPEARE LIBRARY
LONDON AND TORONTO:
ASSOCIATED UNIVERSITY PRESSES

Associated University Presses
440 Forsgate Drive
Cranbury, N. J. 08512

Associated University Presses
25 Sicilian Avenue
London WC1A 2QH, England

Associated University Presses
2133 Royal Windsor Drive
Unit 1
Mississauga, Ontario
Canada L5J 1K5

**Library of Congress Cataloging in Publication Data**
Main entry under title:

Two early Renaissance bird poems.

   "The Renaissance English Text Society and the
Newberry Library."
   Bibliography: p.
   Includes index.
   1. English poetry—Early modern, 1500–1700.   2. Birds
—Poetry.   I. Andrew, Malcolm.   II. Renaissance English
Text Society.   III. Newberry Library.   IV. Title:
2 early Renaissance bird poems.
PR1195.B5T8   1984        821'.2'08036        83-48646
ISBN 0-918016-73-8

Printed in the United States of America

# Contents

# Acknowledgments

DURING THE PREPARATION OF THIS BOOK I HAVE BENE-
fitted greatly from the assistance and encouragement of
Professor A. S. G. Edwards, who supported the project
from its inception and contributed many valuable ideas.

Professors David Bevington, Christina von Nolcken,
and W. Speed Hill read an earlier draft, and the final ver-
sion incorporates a number of their helpful suggestions.

My thanks are also due to the following: the Very
Referend David Edwards, former dean of Norwich Cathe-
dral, and Father Patrick Rorke, S.J., of Oscott College, who
advised me on several biblical and liturgical points; Mr.
Carey F. Bliss of the Huntington Library, who supplied me
with a microfilm of *The Harmony of Birds*; Miss Katharine F.
Pantzer of the Houghton Library, Harvard University, and
Mr. Victor Morgan of the University of East Anglia, Nor-
wich, who answered specific questions; and my wife,
Lena, who gave invaluable help with various phases of the
project.

Finally I wish to record my indebtedness to the staffs of
the libraries in which I worked: the British Library, the
Cambridge University Library, and the library of my own
university, the University of East Anglia, Norwich.

# Abbreviations

FOR FULL REFERENCES TO BOOKS AND ARTICLES, SEE BIBLI-
ography. The title of each book or article listed here is
followed by an indication of the section of the Bibliogra-
phy in which it appears.

| | |
|---|---|
| *Archiv* | *Archiv für das Studium der neueren Sprachen und Literaturen* |
| Armstrong | Edward A. Armstrong, *The Folklore of Birds* (III.B) |
| Bartholomaeus | Bartholomaeus, *On the Properties of Things* (III.A) |
| Chaucer, *CT* | Chaucer, *The Canterbury Tales* (references to Robinson's edition: II.A) |
| Chaucer, *PF* | Chaucer, *The Parliament of Fowls* |
| *ChauR* | *Chaucer Review* |
| *CJ* | *Classical Journal* |
| *CL* | *Comparative Literature* |
| *DUJ* | *Durham University Journal* |
| Dunbar, *Thistle* | Dunbar, *The Thistle and the Rose* |
| *ELH* | *ELH: A Journal of English Literary History* |
| *ELN* | *English Language Notes* |
| Hands | Rachel Hands, ed. *English Hawking and Hunting* (III.A) |
| Hare | C. E. Hare, *Bird Lore* (III.B) |
| *HB* | *The Harmony of Birds* (I.A) |
| *IMEV* | Carleton Brown and Rossell Hope Rob-bins, *The Index of Middle English Verse* (V) |

| | |
|---|---|
| Isidore | Isidore, *Etymologiae* (III.A) |
| *JEGP* | *Journal of English and Germanic Philology* |
| Knortz | Karl Knortz, *Die Vögel* (III.B) |
| Lack | David Lack, *Robin Redbreast* (III.B) |
| Lydgate, *Churl* | Lydgate, *The Churl and the Bird* |
| Lydgate, *Cok* | Lydgate, *The Cok hath Lowe Shoone* |
| Lydgate, *MP* | Henry Noble MacCracken, ed., *The Minor Poems of John Lydgate* (II.A) |
| McCulloch | Florence McCulloch, *Mediaeval Latin and French Bestiaries* (III.B) |
| Maplet | John Maplet, *A Greene Forest* (III.A) |
| Martin | Ernest Whitney Martin, *The Birds of the Latin Poets* (III.B) |
| *MED* | *The Middle English Dictionary* (V) |
| *MLR* | *Modern Language Review* |
| *MP* | *Modern Philology* |
| *MS* | *Mediaeval Studies* |
| *NM* | *Neuphilologische Mitteilungen* |
| N.S. | New Series |
| OE | Old English |
| *OED* | *The Oxford English Dictionary* (V) |
| OF | Old French |
| ON | Old Norse |
| *PB* | *The Parliament of Birds* (I.A) |
| *PBSA* | *Papers of the Bibliographical Society of America* |
| Phipson | Emma Phipson, *The Animal-Lore of Shakespeare's Time* (III.B) |
| *PL* | *Patrologia Latina*, ed. J.-P. Migne (V) |
| Pliny, *NH* | Pliny, *Naturalis Historia* (III.A) |
| *PMLA* | *Publications of the Modern Language Association of America* |
| *PQ* | *Philological Quarterly* |
| *QJS* | *Quarterly Journal of Speech* |
| Randall | Lilian M. C. Randall, *Images in the Margins of Gothic Manuscripts* (III.B) |
| *RES* | *Review of English Studies* |
| *RLC* | *Revue de Littérature Comparée* |

| | |
|---|---|
| Robin | P. Ansell Robin, *Animal Lore in English Literature* (III.B) |
| Rowland | Beryl Rowland, *Birds with Human Souls* (III.B) |
| *RR* | *Romanic Review* |
| Skelton, *PS* | Skelton, *Philip Sparrow* |
| Skelton, *SP* | Skelton, *Speak, Parrot* |
| *SMC* | *Studies in Medieval Culture* |
| *SP* | *Studies in Philology* |
| *STC* | A. W. Pollard and G. R. Redgrave, *A Short-Title Catalogue* (V) |
| Swainson | Charles Swainson, *Provincial Names . . . of British Birds* (III.B) |
| Swann | H. Kirke Swann, *Dictionary of . . . Folk-Names of British Birds* (III.B) |
| *TD* | *Te Deum* |
| de Thaun | Philippe de Thaun, "Bestiary," in Thomas Wright, ed. *Popular Treatises* (III.A) |
| Tilley | Morris Palmer Tilley, *A Dictionary of Proverbs* (V) |
| Topsell | Edward Topsell, *The Fowles of Heauen*, ed. Thomas P. Harrison and F. David Hoeniger (III.A) |
| *TPAPA* | *Transactions and Proceedings of the American Philological Association* |
| Turner | William Turner. *Turner on Birds*, ed. A. H. Evans (III.A) |
| White | T. H. White, Trans. and ed. *The Book of Beasts* (III.A) |
| Whiting | Bartlett Jere Whiting, *Proverbs, Sentences, and Proverbial Phrases* (V) |
| *YES* | *Yearbook of English Studies* |

# Bibliography

THE BIBLIOGRAPHY IS ARRANGED IN SECTIONS AS FOL-
lows:

I. HB *and* PB
    A. TEXTS
        1. *HB*
        2. *PB*
    B. SECONDARY MATERIAL
II. *Other literature*
    A. TEXTS
    B. SECONDARY MATERIAL
III. *Bird lore, including bird lore in literature*
    A. TEXTS
    B. SECONDARY MATERIAL
IV. *Liturgy*
    A. TEXTS
    B. SECONDARY MATERIAL
V. *Miscellaneous reference*

## I. HB *and* PB

A. TEXTS

1. *HB*

*A Proper New Boke of the Armonye of Byrdes.* London: John Wyght,
    c. 1555.

Collier, J. Payne, ed. *The Harmony of Birds: A Poem.* . . . Percy
    Society, vol. 7. London: Percy Society, 1843.

Hazlitt, W. Carew, ed. *Remains of the Early Popular Poetry of England*, 3:184–99. (For full details, see section II.A).

Chandler, Albert R., ed. *Larks, Nightingales and Poets*, 96: text of *HB*, lines 1–36, 72–102. (For full details, see section III.B).

## 2. *PB*

[*The Parlyament of Byrdes*]. London: Wynkyn de Worde, c. 1520.

*The Parlament of Byrdes.* British Library MS. Lansdowne 210, ff. 74–78ᵛ (c. 1560).

*The Parlament of Byrdes.* London: Antony Kytson, c. 1565.

"The Parlement of Byrdes," *Harleian Miscellany* 5 (1745): 479–82. Reprint. *Harleian Miscellany* 5 (1810): 507–10. (Based on the lost edition of Abraham Veale).

Hazlitt, W. Carew, ed. *Remains of the Early Popular Poetry of England*, 3:164–83. (For full details, see section II.A).

### B. SECONDARY MATERIAL

Edwards, A. S. G. "Variant Texts of *The Parliament of Birds*," *PBSA* 69 (1975): 77–79.

## II. *Other Literature*

### A. TEXTS

Alexander, Peter, ed. *William Shakespeare: the Complete Works.* London: Collins, 1951.

Atkins, J. W. H., ed. *The Owl and the Nightingale.* Cambridge: Cambridge University Press, 1922.

Bond, R. Warwick, ed. *The Complete Works of John Lyly.* 3 vols. Oxford: Clarendon Press, 1902.

Brewer, D. S., ed. *Geoffrey Chaucer, The Parlement of Foulys.* London: Nelson, 1960.

Dickins, Bruce, and R. M. Wilson, eds. *Early Middle English Texts.* 3d rev. ed. London: Bowes, 1956. (Includes *The Thrush and the Nightingale*).

Gardner, John, trans. *The Alliterative Morte Arthure, The Owl and the Nightingale, and five other Middle English Poems.* Carbondale: Southern Illinois University Press, 1971. (Also includes *The Thrush and the Nightingale*).

Halliwell, J. O., ed. *Early English Miscellanies, in prose and verse, selected from an inedited manuscript of the fifteenth century.* London: Warton Club, 1855. (Includes *The Poet and the Bird*, 1–6).

Hammond, Eleanor Prescott, ed. "A Parliament of Birds." *JEGP* 6 (1907): 105–9. (Contains *The Birds' Praise of Love*).

———. "The Lover's Mass." *JEGP* 7 (1908): 95–104.

———. *English Verse between Chaucer and Surrey*. Durham, N.C.: Duke University Press, 1927. (Includes *The Lover's Mass* and Lydgate's *Churl*).

Hazlitt, W. Carew, ed. *Remains of the Early Popular Poetry of England*. 4 vols. London: Smith, 1864–66. (Includes *HB, PB*, and *The Thrush and the Nightingale*).

Hebel, J. William, ed. *The Works of Michael Drayton*. 5 vols. corrected ed. Oxford: Blackwell, 1961.

Kinsley, James, ed. *The Poems of Williams Dunbar*. Oxford: Clarendon Press, 1979.

Kinsman, Robert S., *John Skelton: Poems*. Oxford: Clarendon Press, 1969.

Lenaghan, R. T., ed *Caxton's Aesop*. Cambridge: Harvard University Press, 1967.

MacCracken, Henry Noble, ed. *The Minor Poems of John Lydgate*. London: Oxford University Press, 1911, 1934. (Early English Text Society, Extra Series, vols. 107, 192).

———. "Lydgatiana: IV. Unprinted texts from MS. Trinity College, Cambridge, R.3.21," *Archiv* 130 (1913): 286–311. (Includes *The Birds' Devotions*, under the title *The Birds' Matins*, 310–11).

Munsterberg, Peggy, ed. *The Penguin Book of Bird Poetry*. London: Lane/Penguin, 1980.

Robbins, Rossell Hope, ed. *Secular Lyrics of the XIVth and XVth Centuries*. 2d ed. Oxford: Clarendon Press, 1955.

Robinson, F. N., ed. *The Works of Geoffrey Chaucer*. 2d ed. Boston: Houghton Mifflin, 1957.

Scattergood, V. J., ed. *The Works of Sir John Clanvowe*. [Cambridge]: Brewer, 1975. (Includes *The Book of Cupid*).

Sélincourt, Ernest de, and J. C. Smith, eds. *The Poetical Works of Edmund Spenser*. 3 vols. Oxford: Clarendon Press, 1909–10.

Skeat, Walter W., ed. *Chaucerian and Other Pieces*. London: Oxford University Press, 1897. (Supplement to *The Complete Works of Geoffrey Chaucer*).

Stanley, Eric Gerald, ed. *The Owl and the Nightingale*. corrected ed. London: Nelson, 1962.

Stuart, John, ed. "The Editor's Preface" (to the "Chronicles of Aberdeen"). *The Miscellany of the Spalding Club* 2 (1842): xxvii–xxviii. (Contains *The Nightingale and the Kind Child*).

Wells, John Edwin, ed. *The Owl and the Nightingale*. rev. ed. Boston: Heath, 1909.

Wright, Thomas, ed. *The Latin Poems commonly attributed to Walter Mapes*. London: Camden Society, 1841.

### B. SECONDARY MATERIAL

Berdan, John M. *Studies in Tudor Literature: Early Tudor Poetry 1485–1547*. New York: Macmillan, 1920.

Bossy, Michel-André Raoul, "The Prowess of Debate: A Study of a Literary Mode, 1100–1400." Ph.D. diss., Yale University, 1970.

Brewer, D. S. "The Genre of the *Parlement of Fowles*." MLR 53 (1958): 321–26.

Cowgill, Bruce Kent. "The *Parlement of Foules* and the Body Politic." *JEGP* 74 (1975): 315–35.

Faral, Edmond. "Les débats du clerc et du chevalier dans la littérature des XIIᵉ et XIIIᵉ siècles." *Romania* 41 (1912): 473–517.

Hanford, James Holly. "Classical Eclogue and Mediaeval Debate." *RR* 2 (1911): 16–31, 129–43.

———. "The Mediaeval Debate between Wine and Water." *PMLA* 28 (1913): 315–67.

———, and John Marcellus Steadman, Jr., eds. "*Death and Liffe*: An Alliterative Poem." *SP* 15 (1918): 223–94. (The introduction includes a useful review of debate poetry.)

Hedberg, Betty Nye. "The *Bucolics* and the Medieval Poetical Debate." *TPAPA* 75 (1944): 47–67.

Hervieux, Léopold. *Les Fabulistes latins depuis le siècle d' Auguste jusqu'à la fin du moyen âge*. 5 vols. Paris: Firmin–Didot, 1883–99.

Hilgers, Sister Mary. "A Study of the Middle English Bird Debate: Backgrounds, Form, Matter, and Characterization." Ph.D. diss., Notre Dame University, 1972.

Hirzel, Rudolf. *Der Dialog: ein Literarhistorischer Versuch*. 2 vols. Leipzig: S. Hirzel, 1895. Reprint. Hildesheim: Olms, 1963.

Huganir, Kathryn. *The Owl and the Nightingale: Sources, Date, Author*. Philadelphia: University of Pennsylvania Press, 1931.

Hume, Kathryn. *The Owl and the Nightingale: The Poem and Its Critics*. Toronto: Toronto University Press, 1975.

Jeanroy, Alfred. *Les Origines de la Poésie Lyrique en France au Moyen Age*. 4th ed. Paris: Champion, 1969.

———. *La Poésie Lyrique des Troubadours*. 2 vols. Toulouse: Privat; Paris: Didier, 1934.

Kelley, Michael R. "Antithesis as the Principle of Design in the *Parlement of Foules*." *ChauR* 14 (1979): 61–73.

Lampe, David E. "Tradition and Meaning in *The Cuckoo and the Nightingale*." In *Papers on The Art and Age of Geoffrey Chaucer*, ed. John Gardner and Nicholas Joost, 49–62. Carbondale: Southern Illinois University Press, 1967.

———. "Middle English Debate Poems: A Genre Study," Ph.D. diss., University of Nebraska, 1969.

———. "Country Matters and Courtly Eyes: Two Thirteenth Century Middle English Debate Poems." In *ACTA*, vol. 3: *The Thirteenth Century*, ed. Kathleen Ashley, 79–93. Binghamton: State University of New York at Binghamton, 1976. (Includes discussion of *The Thrush and the Nightingale*).

Lumiansky, R. M. "Concerning *The Owl and the Nightingale*." *PQ* 32 (1953): 411–17.

Mason, H. A. *Humanism and Poetry in the Early Tudor Period: An Essay*. London: Routledge, 1959.

Merrill, Elizabeth. *The Dialogue in English Literature*. New York: Holt, 1911.

Neilson, William Allan. *The Origins and Sources of the "Court of Love."* Boston: Ginn, 1899.

Owen, Lewis J. "*The Thrush and the Nightingale:* The Speaker in Lines 94–96." *ELN* 7 (1969): 1–6.

Oulmont, Charles. *Les Débats du Clerc et du Chevalier dans la Littérature Poétique du Moyen Age*. Paris: Champion, 1911.

Pellegrini, Angelo M. "Renaissance and Medieval Antecedents of Debate." *QJS* 28 (1942): 14–19.

Pieper, Wily. "Das Parlament in der m.e. Literatur." *Archiv* 146 (1923): 187–212.

Raby, F. J. E. *A History of Secular Latin Poetry in the Middle Ages*. 2d ed. 2 vols. Oxford: Clarendon Press, 1957.

Reiss, Edmund. "Conflict and Its Resolution in Medieval Dialogues." In *Arts Libéraux et Philosophie au Moyen Age*, 863–72. Montreal: Institut d'Etudes Médiévales; Paris: Vrin, 1969.

Rios, Gladys Wenzel. "The Middle English Poetic Debate: A Definition of Genre." Ph.D. diss., Denton: Texas Woman's University, 1973.

Rutherford, Charles S. *"The Boke of Cupide* Reopened." *NM* 78 (1977): 350–58.

Sandison, Helen Estabrook. *The "Chanson d' Aventure" in Middle English*. Bryn Mawr: Bryn Mawr College, 1913.

Schleusener, Jay. *"The Owl and the Nightingale:* A Matter of Judgment." *MP* 70 (1973): 185–89.

Seelmann, W. "Die Vogelsprachen (Vogelparlamente) der mittelalterlichen Literatur." *Jahrbuch des Vereins für niederdeutsche Sprachforschung* 14 (1888): 101–47.

Tucker, Samuel Marion. *Verse-Satire in England before the Renaissance*. New York: Columbia University Press, 1908.

Walther, H. *Das Streitgedicht in der lateinischen Literatur des Mittelalters*. München: Beck, 1920.

Wimsatt, James. *Chaucer and the French Love Poets: the Literary Background of the "Book of the Duchess."* Chapel Hill: University of North Carolina Press, 1968.

Wright, C. E. "Late Middle English Parerga in a School Collection." *RES* N.S. 2 (1951): 114–20.

## III. Bird lore, including bird lore in literature

### A. TEXTS

Aldrovandi, Ulisse. *Ornithologiae, hoc est de Avibvs Historiae, libri XII.* 3 vols. Bononiae: Senensem, 1599–1603.

Bartholomaeus. *On the properties of Things: John Trevisa's translation of "Bartholomaeus Anglicus De Proprietatibus Rerum": A Critical Text.* 2 vols. Oxford: Clarendon Press, 1975.

Belon, Pierre. *L' Histoire de la Nature des Oyseavx.* Paris: Cauellat, 1555.

Evans, A. H. *see* William Turner.

Gesner, Konrad. *Historiae Animalium liber III qui est de Auium Natura.* Tigvri: Froschoverum, 1555.

Hands, Rachel, ed. *English Hawking and Hunting in "The Boke of St. Albans."* London: Oxford University Press, 1975.

Harrison, Thomas P., and F. David Hoeniger, eds. *The Fowles of Heauen or History of Birdes by Edward Topsell.* Austin: University of Texas Press, 1972.

Isidore of Seville. *see* W. M. Lindsay.

James, M. R., ed. *The Bestiary.* Oxford: Roxburghe Club, 1928.

Lindsay, W. M., ed. *Isidori Hispalensis Episcopi Etymologiarvm sive originvm libri xx.* 2 vols. Oxford: Clarendon Press, 1911.

Maplet, John. *A Greene Forest, or a naturall History.* 1567. Reprint with intro. by W. H. Davies. London: Hesperides Press, 1930.

Millar, Eric George, ed. *A Thirteenth Century Bestiary in the Library of Alnwick Castle.* Oxford: Roxburghe Club, 1958.

Pliny. *see* H. Rackham.

Rackham, H., ed. and trans. *Pliny: Natural History.* 10 vols. Cambridge: Harvard University Press, 1938–63.

de Thaun, Philippe. *see* Thomas Wright.

Topsell, Edward, *see* Thomas P. Harrison and F. David Hoeniger.

Turner, William. *Avivm Praecipvarvm, qvarvm apvd Plinivm et Aristotelem mentio est, breuis & succincta historia.* 1544. Reprint as *Turner on Birds,* ed. A. H. Evans. Cambridge. Cambridge University Press, 1903.

White, T. H., trans. and ed. *The Book of Beasts: Being a Translation of a Latin Bestiary of the Twelfth Century.* London: Cape, 1954.

Wright, Thomas, ed. "The Bestiary of Philippe de Thaun." In his *Popular Treatises on Science written during the Middle Ages in Anglo-Saxon, Anglo-Norman, and English.* London: Taylor, 1841.


B. SECONDARY MATERIAL

Allen, Don Cameron. "Vaughan's 'Cock-Crowing' and the Tradition." *ELH* 21 (1954): 94–106.

Armstrong, Edward A. *The Folklore of Birds: An Enquiry into the Origin & Distribution of some Magico-Religious Traditions.* London: Collins, 1958.

Bawcutt, Priscilla. "The Lark in Chaucer and Some Later Poets." *YES* 2 (1972): 5–12.

Chandler, Albert R. "The Nightingale in Greek and Latin Poetry." *CJ* 30 (1934): 78–84.

———. *Larks, Nightingales and Poets: An Essay and an Anthology.* Columbus, Ohio: privately printed at Ohio State University Press [1938].

Donovan, Mortimer J. "*Sir Thopas, 772–774.*" *NM* 57 (1956): 237–46. (Discusses the thrush in medieval tradition).

Dyer, T. F. Thiselton. *Folk Lore of Shakespeare.* London: Griffith and Farran, 1884.

Evans, E. P. *Animal Symbolism in Ecclesiastical Architecture.* London: Heinemann, 1896.

Fisher, A. S. T. "Birds of Paradise. *Notes and Queries* 188 (1945): 95–98.

Giffin, Mary. "The Pekok with His Aungels Fetheres Bryghte." In her *Studies on Chaucer and His Audience*, 49–66. Quebec: Editions L'Eclair, 1956.

Graham, Victor E. "The Pelican as Image and Symbol." *RLC* 36 (1962): 235–43.

Hagman, Lynn Wells. "Youth and Crabbed Thrush." *SMC* 2 (1966): 71–74. (On *The Thrush and the Nightingale*).

Hare, C. E. *Bird Lore.* London: Country Life, 1952.

Harrison, Thomas Perrin. *Drayton's Birds.* Austin: University of Texas Press, 1950.

————. *They Tell of Birds: Chaucer, Spenser, Milton, Drayton.* Austin: University of Texas Press, 1956.

Harting, James Edmund. *The Ornithology of Shakespeare. Critically examined, explained, and illustrated.* London: Van Voorst, 1871.

Hensel, Werner. "Die Vögel in der provenzalischen und nordfranzösischen Lyrik in der Mittelalters." *Romanischen Forschungen* 26 (1908): 584–670.

Hinckley, Henry Barrett. "Science and Folk-Lore in *The Owl and the Nightingale*." *PMLA* 47 (1932): 303–14.

Knortz, Karl. *Die Vögel in Geschichte, Sage, Brauch und Literatur.* München: Seybold, 1913.

Kreisler, Nicolai von. "Bird Lore and the Valentine's Day Tradition in Chaucer's *Parlement of Foules*." *ChauR* 3 (1968): 60–64.

Lack, David. *Robin Redbreast.* Oxford: Clarendon Press, 1950.

McCulloch, Florence. *Mediaeval Latin and French Bestiaries.* Rev. ed. Chapel Hill: University of North Carolina Press, 1962.

Martin, Ernest Whitney. *The Birds of the Latin Poets.* Stanford: Stanford University Press, 1914.

Newton, Alfred, assisted by Hans Gadow. *A Dictionary of Birds.* London: Black, 1896

Phipson, Emma. *The Animal-Lore of Shakespeare's Time: including quadrupeds, birds, reptiles, fish and insects.* London: Kegan Paul, 1883.

Raby, F. J. E. "Philomena praevia temporis amoeni." In *Mélanges Joseph de Ghellinck, S. J.* 2 vols., 2:435–48. Gembloux: Duculot, 1951.

Randall, Lilian M. C. *Images in the Margins of Gothic Manuscripts.* Berkeley and Los Angeles: University of California Press, 1966.

Robin, P. Ansell. *Animal Lore in English Literature.* London: Murray, 1932.

Robinson, Phil. *The Poet's Birds.* London: Chatto, 1883.

Rowland, Beryl. "Chaucer's 'Throstil Old' and Other Birds." *MS* 24 (1962): 381–84.

———. *Blind Beasts: Chaucer's Animal World.* Kent, Ohio: Kent State University Press, 1971.

———. *Birds with Human Souls: A Guide to Bird Symbolism.* Knoxville: University of Tennessee Press, 1978.

Shippey, Thomas Alan. "Listening to The Nightingale." *CL* 22 (1970): 46–60.

Svendsen, Kester. *Milton and Science.* Cambridge: Harvard University Press, 1956.

Swainson, Charles. *Provincial Names and Folk Lore of British Birds.* London: Trübner, 1885. (English Dialect Society, 47). Reprint as *The Folk Lore and Provincial Names of British Birds.* London: Elliot Stock, 1886. (Publications of the Folk-Lore Society, 17).

Swann, H. Kirke. *Dictionary of English and Folk-Names of British Birds.* London: Witherby, 1913.

Telfer, J. M. "The Evolution of a Mediaeval Theme." *DUJ,* N.S. 14 (1952): 25–34.

Tristam, H. B. *The Natural History of the Bible.* London: S.P.C.K., 1887.

Vinycomb, John. *Fictitious and Symbolic Creatures in Art, with Special Reference to their Use in British Heraldry.* London: Chapman and Hall, 1906.

White, Beatrice. "Medieval Animal Lore." *Anglia* 72 (1954): 21–30.

Wright, Thomas. *A History of Caricature and Grotesque in Literature and Art.* London: Virtue Bros., 1865. Reprint with intro. and index by Frances K. Barasch. New York: Ungar, 1968.

Yapp, Brunsdon. *Birds in Medieval Manuscripts.* London: British Library, 1981.

## IV. Liturgy

### A. TEXTS

*Portiforium seu Breuiarium ad vsum insignis ecclesie Sarum.* 2 vols. N.p.: Iehan Petit, 1528.

*Portiforium secundum vsum Sarum.* 2 vols. London: Edward Whytchurch, 1541.

*The Roman Breviary.* Trans. John, Marquess of Bute. 2 vols. Edinburgh: Blackwood, 1879.

### B. SECONDARY MATERIAL

Podhradsky, Gerhard. *New Dictionary of the Liturgy.* London: Chapman, 1967.

Wordsworth, Christopher, and Henry Littlehales. *The Old Service-Books of the English Church.* London: Methuen, 1904.

## V. Miscellaneous reference

Brown, Carleton, and Rossell Hope Robbins. *The Index of Middle English Verse.* New York: Columbia University Press for the Index Society, 1943. Rossell Hope Robbins and John L. Cutler. *Supplement to the Index of Middle English Verse.* Lexington: University of Kentucky Press, 1965.

Cruden, Alexander. *Cruden's Complete Concordance To the Old and New Testaments.* Ed. C. H. Irwin, A. D. Adams, and S. A. Waters. rev. ed. London: Lutterworth Press, 1954.

*Middle English Dictionary.* Ed. Hans Kurath, Sherman M. Kuhn, and John Reidy. Ann Arbor: University of Michigan Press, 1954–.

Migne, J.-P., ed. *Patrologiae Cursus Completus. Series Latina.* 221 vols. Paris: Garnier, 1878–80.

*The Oxford English Dictionary.* Ed. James A. H. Murray et al. 12 vols. and supplement. rev. ed. Oxford: Clarendon Press, 1933. *Supplement.* Ed. R. W. Burchfield. Oxford: Clarendon Press, 1972–.

Pollard, A. W., and G. R. Redgrave. *A Short-Title Catalogue of Books Printed in England, Scotland, and Ireland.* London: Oxford University Press for the Bibliographical Society, 1926. 2d ed. Revised by W. A. Jackson, F. S. Ferguson, and Katharine F. Pantzer. Vol. 2. London: Bibliographical Society, 1976.

Severs, J. Burke, and Albert E. Hartung, eds. *A Manual of Writings in Middle English 1050–1500.* New Haven: Connecticut Academy of Arts and Sciences, 1967–.

Tilley, Morris Palmer. *A Dictionary of Proverbs in England in the Sixteenth and Seventeenth Centuries.* Ann Arbor: University of Michigan Press, 1950.

Whiting, Barlett Jere, with Helen Wescott Whiting. *Proverbs, Sentences, and Proverbial Phrases From English Writings Mainly Before 1500*. Cambridge: Belknap Press/Harvard University Press; London: Oxford University Press,1968.

# Introduction

*THE HARMONY OF BIRDS* AND *THE PARLIAMENT OF BIRDS*[1] have never been well known to the scholarly community: neither has previously appeared in a critical edition, and such editions as exist have long been out of print. Thus the primary aim of this volume is to present reliable and adequately annotated texts.

## Texts

*HB* exists in an edition printed by John Wight, c. 1555, of which the only known copy is preserved in the Huntington Library.[2] It was reprinted during the nineteenth century by J. Payne Collier for the Percy Society and by W. Carew Hazlitt in his *Remains of the Early Popular Poetry of England;* an extract was included by Albert R. Chandler in his *Larks, Nightingales and Poets.*[3] No additional firm evidence is available to help establish the date of composition. Other, possibly earlier, printed editions may have existed; furthermore, some roughly contemporary poems (e.g., Heywood's *The Spider and the Fly*) were written twenty or more years before they were printed. Taking these two points into consideration along with the general nature and manner of the poem, one might conclude that the date of composition would lie between the years 1530 and 1555. There is little evidence to indicate provenance. The only relevant allusion in the text is the Robin's mention of Sarum use (line 140). Since this use prevailed throughout the country except for the North and a small area around Hereford, the allusion serves only to suggest that *HB* was not written in either of these regions.[4]

*PB* survives in three sixteenth-century texts: an edition printed by de Worde c. 1520, another printed by Kitson c. 1565, and a manuscript version contained in British Library MS. Lansdowne 210, which was copied after the accession of Mary Tudor.[5] A fourth sixteenth-century text, the lost edition printed by Veale, is preserved in the reprint published in the *Harleian Miscellany* of 1745 (and again in the same series in 1810). Hazlitt included *PB* in his *Remains of the Early Popular Poetry of England.* The general style and character of the poem would suggest that it was written at the end of the fifteenth or the beginning of the sixteeth century. If line 70 is understood to contain a reference to the fate of Lambert Simnel,[6] then *PB* could not have been written before 1487. Thus a dating of c. 1487–1520 would seem reasonable. The text contains one possible indication of provenance. In line 193, the titmouse speaks of "we Kentysshe men," or in the Lansdowne versin, "the Norfolk men." Though by no means conclusive, this reference may, in the absence of other evidence, suggest a possible provenance for both *PB* and the version preserved in the Lansdowne MS.

## Literary Background

Extravagant claims for literary excellence on behalf of either *HB* or *PB* would be inappropriate. However, acknowledging the limitations of these poems when judged by aesthetic criteria is far from dismissing them as unworthy of attention: in terms of form and genre, of ideas expressed and attitudes reflected, both are of very considerable interest. It seems likely that they were written for an audience which may loosely be termed "middle class"—probably ecclesiastical in the case of *HB,* clearly secular in the case of *PB.* Thus we have here two specimens of non-courtly minor poetry dating from the early

years of the English Renaissance. As such, the most im-
mediately striking feature of *HB* and *PB* is their conserva-
tism: their use of the bird debate convention which links
them is formulaic rather than experimental; their mode is
predictable, their structure unoriginal, their outlook de-
cidedly conventional. Whatever their virtues, they mani-
festly do not exemplify the bold innovation and growing
individualism which characterizes much of the best
shorter poetry written during the English Renaissance. In-
deed, to appreciate the formal and generic context in
which *HB* and *PB* were written, it is necessary briefly to
review two major medieval traditions.

The first of these is debate as a literary form. This
genre—developed from the classical tradition of poetical
debate, and perhaps also influenced by the classical ec-
logue—emerged as a distinct type during the early Middle
Ages and remained popular well into the Renaissance.[7]
Throughout this period, one encounters debates between
such figures as Wine and Water, the Body and the Soul,
Winter and Summer, and the Heart and the Eye, written in
both Latin and a wide range of vernaculars. The definitive
characteristic of the debate is the exposition of, and the
portrayal of confrontation between, two (or occasionally
more) distinct entities, characters, values, qualities, or ap-
proaches to a particular matter or to life in general. Thus
the form is inherently flexible. Moreover, in addition to a
virtually unlimited freedom in the conception of his de-
bate, the poet could chose between two broad strategies in
the handling of its conclusion: either leaving the issue un-
resolved or specifying a victor. The more religious and
didactic poems tend to specify a resolution, whereas those
in which the focus of interest is on the process itself rather
than the outcome often do not.

Most of the traditional themes and figures of the debate
genre may be observed in the English poetry of the late
Middle Ages. In addition, a number of new ideas appear
in such works as *Winner and Waster* (c. 1350–60) and *The
Flower and the Leaf* (late fifteenth century). Furthermore,
some poets extend the range of the debate form by adding

an extra voice, as in *The Parliament of the Three Ages* (c. 1370), or voices, as in Chaucer's *Parliament of Fowls*. The titles of both these poems contain the word, "parliament," which will be considered shortly; the latter draws our attention to bird debate, to which we now turn.

A considerable number of bird debates exist in Middle English. These may be divided into three types: those conducted between a bird and a human, those conducted between two birds, and those developed into a parliament. Examples of the first include *The Dialogue between the Poet and the Bird* (c. 1460), *The Nichtingall and the Kynd Cheild* (c. 1500), the two fifteenth-century poems entitled *The Clerk and the Nightingale,* and Lydgate's *The Churl and the Bird.*[8] Among the works which belong to the second category are *The Owl and the Nightingale* (c. 1200), *The Thrush and the Nightingale* (c. 1300), and various works by later poets, such as *The Book of Cupid* (also known as *The Cuckoo and the Nightingale*), attributed to Clanvowe and dated c. 1390, and Dunbar's *The Merle and the Nightingale.*[9] (The third group, bird parliaments, is considered below.) Poetic debates, including bird debates, continue to appear in considerable numbers during the sixteenth century, but the majority of these works are derivative and uninspired.

While each is significantly related to the genre, neither *PB* nor *HB* may be regarded as a poetical debate pure and simple. In the case of *PB*, the relationship is straightforward. The "parliament" is a form of the debate, modified in order to provide a multiplicity of voices and to endow the discussion it encapsulates with a particular structure and a specific set of connotations. In medieval literature it occurs most commonly in the guise of the bird parliament, manifestly the genre to which *PB* belongs.[10] *HB* is less easy to categorize. Though clearly related to a number of forms and topics familiar from medieval poetry—the imitation or parody of divine offices, the bird chorus (which usually functions as only one part of a poem), and the bird service (which sometimes stands alone)[11]—it would be misleading to identify it exclusively as any one of these. The nature and significance of the use of the liturgy in *HB* will be

discussed later; our immediate concern is with its relation-
ship to the bird chorus and service. The essential function
of these two distinct but related forms is to provide a
unified but varied expression of celebration in praise of a
deity—which may be Love, Nature, or the Christian God,
according to the world view of the poem in question. Thus
they share a vital characteristic with the parliament. In all
three the portrayal of a confrontation between two distinct
views is extended to create a medium in which different
voices, in any number, can make their individual contribu-
tions to the discussion of a particular topic. There is, how-
ever, a vital distinction between the parliament on the one
hand and the bird chorus and service on the other.
Whereas in the former the individual voices would typi-
cally be used to articulate tensions and conflicts (as in *PB*),
in the latter they are employed to express varying aspects
of a unified statement of praise (as in *HB*). It seems that
the poet of *HB* has combined features of the bird chorus
and the bird service—together with some highly
significant liturgical material—in a hybrid of his own de-
vising.

The second major tradition which must be considered is
that of bird lore. Specifying the origins and sources of
ideas in such a field is a complex and elusive business—
not least because the relevant material occurs in a variety
of media, including folk lore and fine art as well as the
written word. Nevertheless, it appears that the forms
through which bird lore was most directly influential on
the two poems are the Aesopic fable[12] and scientific (or
pseudoscientific) writing about birds. The influence of the
first is a general one, reflected in tone and purpose, and in
certain story elements in *PB*.[13] The second reached the six-
teenth-century reading public chiefly through encyclope-
dias and bestiaries. Classical and medieval encyclopedias
invariably include comments on a number of particular
birds and sometimes contain a section devoted to birds
exclusively.[14] The bestiary, which developed during the
Middle Ages into a well-defined genre, consists of a series
of brief accounts of particular animals, birds, and fishes,

ranging from the actual or likely to the mythical or utterly fantastic.[15]

By the middle of the sixteenth century, a new form of natural history was developing. Based on accurate reporting of scientific observation, it appears in the writings of Konrad Gesner (the publication of whose *Historiae Animalium* began in 1551), Pierre Belon (who published on fishes and birds during the 1550s), and Ulisse Aldrovandi (whose work on birds was printed at the turn of the century).[16] It would, however, be an oversimplification to distinguish absolutely between the fanciful lore of the classical and medieval encyclopedias and bestiaries and the precise scientific observation of the Renaissance naturalists. Many familiar errors and misconceptions recur in the work of the naturalists, some to continue in currency for another century or more.[17] In any case, the English writers on bird lore during the sixteenth century are not especially meticulous in their observation or innovative in their outlook. They may be represented by William Turner, whose *Avium Principuarum* (1541) takes the form of a commentary on the views of Pliny; by John Maplet, whose natural history, *A Greene Forest,* was published in 1567; and by Edward Topsell, whose work, *The Fowles of Heauen,* is an incomplete translation of Aldrovandi and dates from the early years of the seventeenth century.[18] These writers provide parallels to and explications of many of the ideas expressed or alluded to in *HB* and *PB.*

Literary forms based on or around bird and animal lore tend to be didactic or sententious in nature. The Aesopic fable concerns anthropomorphic beasts and functions specifically to instruct the human audience, while the purpose of the bestiary is to specify the real or imagined attributes of real or imagined creatures in order to achieve the same end. Even encyclopedias, which one might expect to be more objective in tone and function, are often, in fact, overtly didactic.[19] Thus the sententiousness of *HB* and *PB* is hardly surprising. It is achieved variously: in *HB* through the dominant tone of divine praise and the interweaving of liturgical material into the text; in *PB* through

the resolution of conflict in the affirmation of regal power
and the recurring aphoristic and proverbial utterances.

## Form and Theme

HB is a poem of some 330 short lines, arranged in regu-
lar six-line stanzas rhyming *aabccb*. Its most immediately
striking characteristic is the use of macaronic form; be-
tween a quarter and a third of the text is in Latin.[20] The
selection and arrangement of these lines is governed by
one essential principle. Most of them are taken directly
from the *Te Deum*,[21] virtually the whole of which is incor-
porated into the poem, consistently and sequentially[22] HB
also contains a relatively small number of Latin lines from
other sources. Some of these consist of quotations from
various biblical texts; others appear to be lines of the poet's
own, designed mainly to fulfill the demands of the stanza
form or the rhyme scheme.

This fundamental use of the *Te Deum* has the effect of
associating HB with praise and thanksgiving. These asso-
ciations seem entirely appropriate: drawing on the tradi-
tion of the divine service performed by birds, the poet
employs their individual voices to create the impression of
a varied but unified expression of worship. The precise
degree of originality in his use of the *Te Deum* is uncertain.
He may have known Lydgate's *Te Deum Laudamus*,[23] in
which the text of the Latin hymn is employed in a gener-
ally similar fashion—but less consistently, less imagina-
tively, and with less effective results than in HB. However,
he undoubtedly drew on a number of more general tradi-
tions and devices, in addition to those of debate and bird
chorus. Poems based on biblical or liturgical texts are not
uncommon in the late Middle Ages and early Renaissance.
The adoption of the macaronic technique has the effect of
associating HB with the tradition of religious lyrics and
hymns with which it was principally identified. Finally,
the framing device—in which the figure of the poet, wan-
dering abroad on a spring or summer day, happens upon a

leafy arbor—is one which was widely used in the *chansons d'aventure* and the love visions of the later Middle Ages.[24]

In his handling of bird lore, the poet is conservative but selective. The birds themselves represent a mixture of the familiar, the exotic, and the mythical: though common species such as the sparrow, the robin, and the thrush predominate, exotic creatures like the peacock and the pelican are included, as well as the mythical phoenix.[25] There is nothing surprising or innovative about the ideas with which the poet links any particular bird, but he exercised his judgment to good effect both in the selection of birds for inclusion and in the choice of which stock associations to mention. In accord with the poem's theme of praise and harmony, many birds identified with negative values or conflict have been omitted. Thus the cuckoo and the crow, both of which feature in *PB*, are absent. Similarly, when the ideas traditionally connected with a particular bird are mixed, the poet is careful to select those which seem most positive, harmonious, and appropriate to a religious poem; the nightingale therefore sings of divine rather than human love, and we hear about the hawks' majestic flight, not their hunting of smaller birds.[26] The essential structure which he devised for *HB* also obliged the poet to perform a further process of selection and manipulation. He had to choose which verses of the *Te Deum* were to be attributed to which bird—a task accomplished with varying degrees of success. At times, the basic ideas with which a particular bird is commonly associated made the choice virtually automatic, as in the case of the wren (lines 187–98) and of the pelican (lines 211–22). Elsewhere, we encounter a range of effects, including the astute connection between the magpie and the prophets (lines 115–20), the grotesque perception of domestic fowl as martyrs (lines 121–32), and the strained ingenuity which links the migration of the swallows with Christ's departure and subsequent return in the role of judge (lines 235–46). The final impression is of a poem controlled by an ingenious but somewhat restrictive central idea, written by a poet of undoubted competence but decidedly limited range and imagination.

Turning from *HB* to *PB,* one experiences a powerful sense of similarity and contrast. Though the resemblances between the two poems—in terms of mode, form, scale, content, and genre—are obvious, the differences are more immediately striking. While *HB* is a religious poem designed to communicate a sense of harmony, *PB* is a secular poem, which, despite its final message, portrays a great deal of strife. If *HB* is unified almost to the point of stultification, *PB*'s loose construction verges on incoherence. In place of the elevation of *HB*'s macaronic form and the regularity of its neat six-line stanza, *PB* offers plain, colloquial English, together with frequent deviations from its basic (and sometimes rather ragged) four-line stanza. Whereas the limited talent of the author of *HB* results in a tidy but somewhat constricted poem, the slapdash writing of the author of *PB* produces an untidy but lively, and occasionally striking, work.

The use of bird lore in *PB* is broadly similar to that in *HB.*[27] Most of the notions mentioned by the poet are familiar, and he, too, has the task of finding the most appropriate speaker for each phase in his argument.[28] The matching of speaker to statement is, perhaps, done with rather less care in *PB* than in *HB*—the results varying from the completely appropriate to the utterly arbitrary.[29]

In terms of structure and of plot, *PB* gives a palpably composite impression. Three elements may be recognized: the story of the common birds' attempt to restrict the hawk, the story of the crow's borrowed feathers, and some general avian moralizing. The disposition of these within the poem is as follows:

| lines: | 1–152 | story: | hawk |
| --- | --- | --- | --- |
| | 153–76 | | crow |
| | 177–84 | | hawk |
| | 185–254 | | crow |
| | 255–76 | | hawk |

| 277–92 | crow |
| 293–312 | moralizing |

It is difficult to offer a precise judgment of the poet's responsibility for the mixing of these elements. Whereas the final passage of moralizing shows signs of being a relatively recent addition—since it is barely connected with the rest of the poem and not particularly relevant as a summary of the main moral lessons[30]—the stories of the hawk and the crow provide evidence of considerable interweaving, especially in the central part of the poem. This is not to suggest that the integration of the two is sophisticated, or even satisfactory; the connections between them are mostly rudimentary,[31] and shifts in the plot (e.g., at lines 152–53 or 254–55) come more in the form of abrupt lurches than of smooth transitions. Each plot element is a familiar type. The tale of the birds' attempt to curb the activities of the hawk has clear affinities with the mode of the fable, though there is no Aesopic fable on precisely this subject.[32] Narratives very similar to that of the crow's borrowed feathers do, however, exist as fables.[33] In addition, this story has significant elements in common with Chaucer's *Manciple's Tale*, though this should not necessarily be taken as evidence of direct influence; the parallels could well result from independent use of common material. The final passage of moralizing may, at some point in its history, have been modelled on a piece concerning the Seven Deadly Sins, since four of the seven (wrath, sloth, lust, and gluttony) are mentioned or alluded to. But it is unlikely that any more specific source could be discerned for so commonplace a passage. Finally, despite the almost identical titles, there is no evidence that *PB* was directly influenced by Chaucer's *Parliament of Fowls*.

The emphasis upon sharp and genuine differences of opinion is manifest. *PB* portrays two major issues, each generated by the kinds of fears and jealousies which exist in any mixed society—and, indeed, shows a far greater degree of liveliness and subtlety in the examination of these tensions than in the articulation of the rather facile

solutions which are finally offered. In this regard, the link-
ing of the stories of the hawk and the crow seems felici-
tous, since both deal with the theme of social tensions and
jealousies. The discussion of these issues is, on the whole,
pragmatic in tone, though not without philosophical im-
plications or touches of idealism. In the opening ex-
changes (lines 11–46) the various views presented—the
cynical self-seeking of the vulture and the cuckoo, the
somewhat legalistic rectitude of the falcon, the bitter social
criticism in the words of the starling, and the weary resig-
nation in those of the parrot—are unified by the fact that
they all address the issue of individual and corporate free-
dom and responsibility. The poet achieves a sense of con-
tinuity in this debate through his handling of the role of
the hawk. In this part of the poem, as the central character,
he naturally dominates the discussion; but it is striking
and unexpected that he should continue to do so after the
subject has shifted to the crow and the borrowed feathers.
The hawk thus seems to function as a commentator—an
impression intensified by the substantial number of
proverbial utterances which the poet assigns to him. Ad-
mittedly, the poem as a whole is full of proverbs, maxims,
and sententious observations of every kind;[34] but the hawk
gives voice to far more of these than his fair share.

The insistent use of proverbial material and the recur-
rence of the sententious tone not only reflect the poet's
own tastes and predilections, but also suggest that he was
seeking a means of presenting the open discussion and
wise resolution of some particular social issues. This de-
sire to portray the debating and resolution of such prob-
lems is also apparent in his use of the parliamentary
metaphor. By establishing it as the dominant metaphor
from the outset, he provides himself with a very service-
able vehicle for the articulation of his themes: specific, in
that each voice is thus contextualized, yet flexible, in that
there is no evident procedural constraint. Indeed, the poet
does not attempt to follow actual parliamentary procedure
with any precision. Taken together with the general tone
of the debate, this might suggest that *PB* was not written

to comment on particular contemporary events. However, in at least one place there may well be a reference to a celebrated incident from the late fifteenth century,[35] and it remains possible that the persistent obscurity of much of the poem results from the presence of an occasional allegory, not yet discovered. While this issue must be left unresolved, the relationship between *PB* and the genres with which it is most closely associated is clear. The poet combined techniques from the debate tradition with the mode of the fable and the metaphor of the parliament in order to create a congenial medium through which to discuss the social issues which so clearly interested him, while indulging his apparent taste for the aphoristic utterance and the sententious manner.

## Editorial Procedures

Abbreviations in the base texts have been expanded without notice. Word-division and capitalization follow modern practice. Punctuation is editorial. Textual apparatus for both poems is provided in the Textual Notes (pp. 69–76).

The text of *The Harmony of Birds* is based on that of Wight, which is represented by the siglum W. It is necessary to restore a number of words partially lost as a result of damage to the outside edge of the pages in the unique surviving copy. The sense and the rhyme scheme together usually provide a clear indication of what is missing.

The two nineteenth-century texts (Collier and Hazlitt) have no independent value. Neither is particularly accurate, and errors in these texts are not recorded.

Some of the poet's Latin words and phrases cause minor editorial problems. In places where *Te Deum* does not supply him with sufficient material to fill his stanza, the poet will sometimes add phrases and lines of his own composition. The Latin of these is not always accurate or syntactically compatible with the neighboring lines borrowed from *Te Deum* (e.g., in line 290). Practice in such cases has been to emend only where sense or syntax makes it necessary. There are also signs that the Latin has suffered during the process of textual transmission, and a number of basic errors have been corrected (e.g., in line 269).

The apparatus is, therefore, used to record readings from W rejected for reasons of sense or syntax, and readings incomplete as a consequence of the damage to the text. Two emendations which could be considered speculative are adopted. In order to render them conspicuous, they are marked with an asterisk (*).

In preparing an edition of *The Parliament of Birds*, it is necessary to take full account of all four sixteenth century texts. These are represented by the following sigla:

> K   Kitson
> L   Lansdowne
> V   Veale
> W   de Worde

This edition is based on W in lines 33 to 288, and on K in lines 1 to 32 and 289 to 312, where W is lacking. An authoritative account of the relationship between the sixteenth-century texts is provided by Edwards, 1975 (I.B).

Emendations have been made primarily on grounds of sense. Rhyme is too unreliable to provide an adequate basis for emendation, though it can at times supply useful supporting evidence (e.g., in lines 26 and 213). Metre is altogether too uneven to be used as a criterion for emendation.

A twofold apparatus is supplied. The first part lists readings rejected from the base text, together with evidence from the other texts to support or elucidate the emendation. In the few cases in which an emendation is made without such support, it is marked with an asterisk (*). The second part lists substantive variants to the edited text.

## Notes

Each reference to a book or article not included in the table of Abbreviations is followed by an indication of the section of the Bibliography in which it is listed.

1. Hereafter respectively *HB* and *PB*.

2. The estimated date has been kindly provided by Katharine F. Pantzer. This edition will be numbered 3368.2 in the revised *STC*.

3. For full details, see Bibliography, Sections I.A and II.A.

4. See also note to *HB* 140.

5. The dates are those given in the revised *STC*, where the numbers of these editions are: de Worde, 19303.7; Kitson, 19304. For full details of these and the following items, see Bibliography, Section I.A.2.

6. See note to *PB* 70.

7. The standard work on medieval Latin debate poetry is Walther, 1920 (II.B). See also: Bossy, 1970; Hanford, 1911; Hanford, 1913; Hedberg, 1944; Lampe, 1969; Oulmont, 1911; Raby 1957, 2:282–308; Rios, 1973 (all II.B). The question of the influence of the eclogue is a matter on which there has been some disagreement: see Hedberg for a review of the issue.

8. *The Nichtingall and the Kynd Cheild* is excluded from *IMEV*: see Stuart, 1842 (II.A), for the only printed text. The numbers of the other three anonymous poems in *IMEV* are, respectively: 2018, 1452, and *5.

9. The date given here for the composition of *The Owl and the Nightingale* is intended only as an approximate guide, since the precise date is disputed. *The Thrush and the Nightingale* is *IMEV*, 3222.

10. A survey of bird parliaments is provided in Seelmann, 1888 (II.B).

11. For example: imitation of the mass occurs in *The Lovers' Mass* (*IMEV*, 4186), and of the requiem mass in Skelton, *PS*; parody of matins and lauds occurs in *The Court of Love* (*IMEV*, 4205). Bird choruses appear in many poems, including *The Birds' Devotions* (*IMEV*, 357), *The Flower and the Leaf* (*IMEV*, 4026), and Dunbar, *Thistle*. Birds perform a religious service in Jean de Condé's *La Messe des Oisiaus*, *The Birds' Devotions*, *The Court of Love*, and Clanvowe's *Book of Cupid*.

12. The standard work on the subject is Hervieux, 1883–99 (II.B).

13. See below, p. 34.

14. For a general survey, see R. Collison, *Encyclopedias: Their History Throughout the Ages*, 2d ed. (New York: Hafner, 1966).

15. A valuable brief survey is provided by White, 1954 (III.B). See also McCulloch.

16. For full details, see Bibliography, Section III.A.

17. For an example, see note to *HB* 241.

18. The works of Turner and Maplet have been reprinted during this century: see Bibliography, Section III.A. Maplet is, in fact, heavily dependent on Trevisa's fourteenth-century translation of the *De Proprietatibus Rerum* of Bartholomaeus Anglicus (c. 1240). Topsell's work was not published during his lifetime and survives in a unique manuscript in the Huntington Library (MS. El. 1142). Despite its not insubstantial scale (248 leaves), it constitutes a translation of only the first three letters of the alphabet from Aldrovandi's prodigious original. The modern reprint, Harrison and Hoeniger, 1972 (III.A), is a somewhat abbreviated version.

19. Thus, for instance, the express purpose of some medieval encyclopaedias is to explicate the scriptures: see e.g., Bartholomaeus, *Prohemium*.

20. No precise line-count is possible, since some of the Latin is in the form of half-lines or single words in otherwise English lines.

21. On the history and interpretation of this hymn, see Podhradsky, 1967 (IV.B), p. 193.

22. Though this point is essential to an understanding of *HB*—and, indeed, seems relatively obvious—it appears to have eluded previous editors and commentators. Latin and English texts of the *Te Deum* are printed in Appendices A and B. The relationship between particular lines of *HB* and the corresponding verses of *Te Deum* is discussed in the notes to the appropriate lines.

23. Printed in Lydgate, *MP*, 1:21–24.

24. See Neilson, 1899, and Sandison, 1913 (both II.B).

25. It is possible that the poet would have thought of the phoenix as exotic rather than mythical. Turner, in relating the traditional stories about the phoenix, states that he is by no means certain whether or not they are true (Turner, p. 140).

26. The treatment of each, especially the hawk, is quite different in *PB*.

27. Although forty-one species are mentioned in *PB*, in contrast to the twenty in *HB*, there is a considerable degree of overlap between the two groups: for particular cases, consult the Index of Bird Names. The poet of *PB* does not include the phoenix and (unlike the poet of *HB*) shows no concern to exclude birds associated with negative ideas.

28. Though he is working on a model considerably less rigid than that employed in *HB*.

29. Thus, for instance, the chough and the cormorant are connected with ideas entirely appropriate to their reputations in bird lore (see lines 145–52 and 227–34), while the use of the peacock and the swan in lines 169–72 seems wholly arbitrary.

30. A full examination of the relationship between the final moralizing passage and the main body of the poem would reveal various inconsistencies. These, in fact, begin a little earlier, in the statement which summarizes the findings of the parliament. For instance, it is unsatisfactory that the raven, who has not previously been mentioned, should be warned (in lines 285–86) against doing something very similar to what the crow has actually done in the story of the borrowed feathers. Similarly, it is curiously inept to use the jay—who, like the raven, has not featured earlier—to endorse an observation which effectively encapsulates the moral of this story (line 190).

31. The exception is the shared theme of social tension, considered below.

32. There are, however, clear parallels both with the fable of the parliament of the animals (retold, for instance, by Henryson), and with that in which the birds elect a king (as, for instance, in Marie de France's *Parlemens des Oiseaux por faire Roi*).

33. There is, for example, a fable in which the bat, once a bird, is stripped of his feathers, and another in which the crow dons the cast-off feathers of a peacock. Evidence of the continuing familiarity of the story of the crow's borrowed feathers is provided by Greene's well-known reference to Shakespeare as "an vpstart Crow, beautified with our feathers" (*The Groatsworth of Wit,* in *The Life and Complete Works in Prose and Verse of Robert Green, M.A.,* ed. Alexander B. Grosart [London: privately printed, 1881–86], 12:144).

34. A characteristic which it shares with some other debate poems, in particular *The Owl and the Nightingale.*

35. See above, p. 26, and *PB* n. 70.

*Two Early Renaissance Bird Poems*

*The Harmony of Birds*

# The Harmony of Birds

Whan Dame Flora,
*In die aurora,*
   Had couerd ye medowes with flowers,
And all the fylde
Was ouer distylde             5
   With lusty Aprell showers,

For my disporte,
Me to conforte,
   Whan the day began to spring,
Foorth I went               10
With a good intent
   To here the byrdes syng.

I was not past,
Not a stones cast,
   So nygh as I could deme,      15
But I dyd se
A goodly tree
   Within an herbor grene,

Wheron dyd lyght
Byrdes as thycke           20
   As sterres in the skye,
Praisyng our Lorde
Without discorde,
   With goodly armony.

The popyngay              25
Than fyrst dyd say,

*"Hoc didicit per me:*
Emperour and kyng
Without lettyng
   *Discite semper a me.* 30

"Therefore wyll I
The name magnify
   Of God aboue all names,"
And fyrst begyn
In praisyng to him 35
   This song, *"Te Deum laudamus."*

Then sang the *auys*
Called the mauys
   The trebble in ellamy,
That from the ground 40
Her notes round
   Were herde into the skye.

Than all the rest,
At her request,
   Both meane, basse, and tenur, 45
With her dyd respond
This glorious song,
   *"Te Dominum confitemur."*

The partryge sayd,
"It may not be denayd 50
   But that I vse my fath
In flood and land,
In erth and sand,
   In hyghway and in path;

"Than with the erth 55
Wyll I make merth,
   Accordyng to my nature."
She tuned then,
*"Te, eternum Patrem,*
   *Omnis terra veneratur."* 60

Than sayd the pecocke,
"All ye well wot
  I syng not musycall,
For my brest is decayd;
Yet I haue," he sayd,                  65
  "Fethers angelicall."

He sang, *"Tibi*
*Omnes angeli,*
  *Tibi celi,"* he dyd reherse,
*"Et vniuersi,*                    70
Sot estates on hye,"
  And so concluded the verse.

Than sayd the nightyngale,
"To make shorte tale,
  For wordes I do refuse,          75
Because my delyght,
Both day and nyght,
  Is syngyng for to vse:

*"Tibi cherubin*
*Et seraphin,"*                  80
  Full goodly she dyd chaunt,
With notes merely
*"Incessabile*
  *Uoce proclamant."*

Than sang the thrusshe,          85
*"Sanctus, sanctus,*
  *Sanctus,"* with a solempne note,
In Latyn thus:
*"Dominus Deus,*
  In Hebrew, *"Sabaoth."*         90

Than sayd the larke,
"Bycause my parte
  Is vpward to ascend,
And downe to rebound,

47

Toward the ground,                                          95
  Singyng to discend;

"Than after my wunt
*Pleni sunt,*
  *Celi  et terra,*" quod she,
"Shall be my song,                                          100
On briefe and long,
  *Maiestatis glorie tue.*"

The cocke dyd say,
"I vse alway
  To crow both fyrst and last;                      105
Like a postle I am,
For I preche to man
  And tell him the nyght is past.

"I bring new tidynges
That the Kyng of all kynges                                 110
  *In tactu profudit chorus*";
Than sang he mellodius,
"*Te gloriosus*
  *Apostolorum chorus.*"

Than sayd the pye,                                          115
"I do prophecye,
  Than may I well syng thus:
*Sub vmbra alarum*
*Te prophetarum*
  *Laudabilis numerus.*"                           120

Than the byrdes all
Domesticall,
  All at once dyd crye,
"For mankyndes sake,
Both erly and late,                                         125
  We be all redy to dye.

*"Te martyrum,*
Both all and sum,"
  They sang mellifluus,
*Candidatus* so bright                 130
One God of myght
  *Laudat exercitus."*

Than the redbrest
His tunes redrest,
  And sayd, "Now wyll I holde     135
With the churche, for there,
Out of the ayere,
  I kepe me from the colde.

*"Te per orbem terrarum,"*
*In vsum Sarum*                   140
  He sange *cum gloria;*
*"Sancta"* was nexte,
And than the hole texte
  *"Confitetur ecclesia."*

Than the egle spake,           145
"Ye know my estate,
  That I am lorde and kyng;
Therfore wyll I
To the father only
  Gyue laude and praisyng."     150

He toke his flyght
To the sonnes lyght,
  *Oculis aura verberatis;*
*"Patrem,"* he sang,
That all the wood rang        155
  *"Immense maiestatis."*

Than sayd the phenix,
"There is none such
  As I, but I alone;

Nor the Father, I proue,                                    160
Reygnyng aboue,
   Hath no mo sonnes but one.

"With tunes mylde
I sang that chylde
   *Uenerandum verum;*                            165
And his name dyd reherse
In the ende of the verse,
   *Et vnicum filium.*"

Than sayd the doue,
"Scripture doth proue                                        170
   That, from the Deite,
The Holy Spiright
On Christ dyd lyght
   In lykenesse of me;

"And syth the Spiright                                       175
From heuen bright
   Lyke vnto me dyd come,
I wyll syng," quod she,
*"Sanctum quoque
Paracletum Spiritum."*                                       180

Than all in one voyce
They dyd all reioyce,
   *Omnes vox iste,*
Chaungyng their key
From vt to rey,                                              185
   *"Et tu rex glorie Christe."*

Then sayd the wren,
"I am called the hen
   Of our Lady most cumly;
Than of her Sun                                              190
My notes shall run,
   For the loue of that lady."

By tytle and ryght
The Son of myght,
   She dyd hym well dyscus,            195
*"Tu Patris"* syngyng,
"Without any endyng,
   *Sempiternus es filius."*

The tyrtle trew,
With notes new,                     200
   The lady of chastyte,
Of a vyrgins wombe
Was all her songe,
   And of mannes lybertye:

*"Tu ad liberandum,*              205
*Et saluandum*
   *Hominem perditum,*
*Non horruisti*
*Sed elegisti*
   *Uirginis uterum."*            210

Than sayd the pellycane,
"Whan my byrdes be slayne,
   With my bloude I them reuyue;
Scrypture doth record
The same dyd our Lord,        215
   And rose from deth to lyue."

She sange, *"Tu deuicto*
*Mortis aculeo,*
   *Ut Dominus dominorum,*
*Tu ascendisti,*            220
*Et apparuisti*
   *Credentibus regna celorum."*

The osyll dyd pricke
Her notes all thycke,
   With blacke ynke and with red;     225

And in lyke facyon
With Christ in his passyon,
   From the fote to the crown of ye hed.

"But now he doth raygne
With his Father agayne,                       230
   *In dextera Maiestatis.*"
Than sang she with ioye,
"*Tu ad dexteram Dei*
   *Sedes, in gloria Patris.*"

The swalowes syng swete,                 235
"To man we be mete,
   For with him we do buylde;
Lyke as from aboue,
God, for mannes loue,
   Was borne of a mayden mylde.        240

"We come and go,
As Christ shall do,
   To iudge both great and small."
They sang for this,
"*Iudex crederis*                    245
   *Esse venturus*" all.

Than in prostracion
They made oration
   To Christ that died vpon the rood,
To haue mercy on those            250
For whom he chose
   To shed his precious blood.

"*Te ergo quesumus,*
We pray the, Iesus,
   *Famulos tuos subueni*          255
*Ab homine doloso,*
*Quos precioso*
   *Sanguine redemisti.*"

The haukes dyd syng,
Their belles dyd ryng;                                    260
   Thei said they came from the tower:
"We hold with the kyng,
And wyll for him syng
   To God—day, nyght, and hower."

The sparrowes dyd tell                                   265
That Christ in his Gospell
   A texte of theym dyd purpose:
"*Suis heredibus,*
*Multis passeribus*
   *Meliores estis vos.*"                       270

They fell downe flat,
With *"Saluum fac*
   *Populum tuum, Domine,*
In heuen to sit,
*Et benedic*                                             275
   *Hereditate tue.*"

Than all dyd respond:
"Lorde, helpe at hond,
   *Ne cadant ad infernum;*
*Et rege eos,*                                           280
*Et extolle illos*
   *Usque in eternum.*"

They toke their flyght,
Prayeng for the ryght,
   And thus their prayer began:                   285
"*Pater noster, qui es* . . .
*Per singulos dies*
   *Benedicimus te,* God and man.

"*Et laudamus*
*Et gloriosus*                                           290
   *Nomen tuum* so hye,

*In seculum* here,
In this militant quere,
   *Et in seculum seculi."*

They dyd begyn                              295
To pray that syn
   Shuld clene from vs *exire:*
*"Dignare Domine,*
*Die isto sine*
   *Peccato nos custodire."*               300

With supplication
They made intercessyon,
   And sang, *"Miserere nostri,"*
Rehersyng this texte
In Englysh nexte,                      305
   "Lorde, on vs haue mercy."

Than dyd they prepare
Away for to fare,
   And all at once arose,
Singyng in a ra,                       310
*"Fiat misericordia tua,*
   *Domine, super nos."*

With tunes renude
They dyd conclude
   Whan they away shuld flye,      315
To syng all and sum,
*"Quemadmodum*
   *Sperauimus in te."*

Than dyd I go
Where I came fro,                   320
   And ever I dyd pretend
Not to tary long,
But of this song
   To make a fynall ende.

I sayd, *"In te, Domine,* 325
*Speraui cotidie,*
   That I fall not *in infernum;*
And than with thy grace,
After this place,
   *Non confundar ineternum.* 330

*The Parliament of Birds*

# The Parliament of Birds

This is the parlyament of byrdes,
For hye and lowe and them amyddes,
To ordayne a meane: how it is best
To keepe among them peace and rest,
For muche noyse is on euery syde                    5
Agaynst the hauke so full of pride.
Therfore they shall in bylles bryng
Theyr complaints to the egle, theyr kyng;
And by the kynge in parlyament
Shall be sette in lawful iudgement.                  10

The great grype was the fyrst that spake,
And sayd, "Owne is owne, who can it take.
For thyne and myne make much debate
Wyth great and small in euery estate."

"I synge," sayd the cuckowe, "euer one song,        15
That the weake taketh euer the wrong,
For he that hath wyth vs most myght
Taketh his wyll, as reason is ryght."

Than answered the fawcon to that saw:
"That pleaseth a prynce is iust and law;            20
And he that can no song but one,
What he hath song his wytte is gone."

Than all the byrdes that could speake
Said, "The hauke doth vs great wreake:
Of them so many diuers there be                     25
That no foule nor byrde may fro them fle."

The hauke answered the prating pye:
"Where is many wordes the trouth goeth by;
And better it were to seace of language sone,
Than speake and repent whan thou hast done."          30

Than sayd the sterlynge: "Verament,
Who sayth soth shal be shent;
No man maye now speke of trouthe
But his heed be broke, and that is routhe."

The hawke swore by his heed of graye:                 35
"All sothes be not for to saye:
It is better some be lefte by reason,
Than trouthe to be spoken out of season."

Than spake the popyngeiay of paradyse:
"Who saythe lytell, he is wyse,                        40
For lytell money is sone spende,
And fewe wordes are sone amende."

The hawke bade: "For drede of payne
Speke not to moche of thy souerayne,
For who that wyll forge tales newe                    45
Whan he weneth leest his tale may rewe."

Than desyred they grete and small
To mewe the hawke for good and all:
"A place alone we wolde he had,
For his counseyll to vs was neuer glad."              50

The hawke answered: "Ye fayle all wyt;
It is not tyme to mewe hawkes yet.
Comyns of hawkes can but lytell skyll:
They shall not reule them as they wyll."

Anone than sange the nyghtyngale,                     55
With notes many grete and smale:
"The byrde that can well speke and synge
Shall be cherysshed with quene and kynge."

The hawke answered with grete fury,
"The songe is nought that is not mery,                60

And whoso no better songe can
Maketh lytell chere to ony man."

Then rombled the douue for her lot:
"Folke may be mery and synge not;
And whoso hath no good voyce                                65
Must make mery with lytell noyse."

Whan this reason was forth shewed,
"Lerne," quod the hawke, "or ye be lewed:
For the byrde that cannot speke ne synge
Shall to the kechyn to serue the kynge."                    70

Than crowed the fesaunt in the wode:
"Dumme men," he sayde, "geteth lytell good,
Wode, ne water, ne other food:
It fleteth from hem as dothe the flode."

The hawke sayd: "Whan all is sought,                        75
Grete crowers were neuer ought;
For I swere the by my foly,
He is not moost wyse that is moost ioly."

Than crowed agayne the morecocke:
"The hawke bryngeth moche thynge out of nocke."             80
The osyll wysteleth and byrdes blake:
"He must haue ado that ado dothe make."

"I must," sayd the hawke, "by all my belles,
Saye for myselfe whan none wyll elles:
He is not gretely to repreue                                85
That speketh with his souerayns leue."

Then blustred the bottore in the fenne,
The cote, the dobchyk, and the waterhenne:
"The hawke, that dothe vs all this dere,
We wolde he were sowsed in the mere."                       90

The hawke sayd: "Wysshers want wyll,
Whether they speke loude or styll;
Whan all this done ys, sayd and lafte,
Euery man must lyue by his crafte."

Than creked the malarde and the gose:    95
"They may best fle that are lose;
He is well that is at large,
That nedeth not the kynges grete charge."

The hawke sayd: "Thoughe they fle lose
They muste obey, they may not chose;    100
Who hathe a mayster or a make,
He is tyed faste by the stake."

Than creked the heron and the crane:
"Grete trouble make wyttes lame;
He is well auysed that can bere hym lowe,    105
And suffre euery wynde to ouerblowe."

The hawke sayd: "Who can blowe to plese
Longe neckes done grete ese;
For the comyns that haue no rest
Meueth not euer with the beste."    110

The pertryche, quayle, and larke in felde
Sayd: "Here may nowght auayle but spere and shelde:
The hawke with vs maketh grete batayle
In euery countre where he maye auayle."

The hawke sayd: "Whoso wylfully wyll fyght    115
May make hym wronge sone of his ryght.
Lawe is best, I vnderstonde,
To ryght all thynge in euery londe."

Than chydde the robyn and the wrenne
And all small byrdes that bereth pen:    120
"Ayenst the hawke the comunes must aryse
And helpe themselfe on theyr best wyse."

The hawke made the wrenne his answere:
"Small power maye lytell dere;
And who wyll lyue in rest longe    125
Maye not be besy with his tonge."

Than prayed all the comyn house
That some myght the hawke sous,
"For foule ne byrde, by water ne londe,

He wyll leaue alyue and he may stonde.                    130
For nere his nest may none abyde
In countre where he dothe glyde:
Theyr fethers he plucketh many a folde
And leueth them naked in full grete colde.
We thynke therfore the reason good                        135
To destroye the hawke and all his blode."

   The kynge and his lordes answered anone:
"States may not the hawke fordone,
Nor by no lawe his kynde destroye,
Nor deme hymselfe for to dye,                             140
Nor put hym to none other dystresse,
But kepe hym in a payre of gesse,
That he fle not to no byrde aboute
But his keper let hym out."

   Than sayd the Cornysshe dawe:                        145
"Lytell money, lytell lawe;
For here is nought elles with frende ne fo
But 'Go bet, peny, go bet, go.' "

   "Thou Cornysshe," quod the hawke, "by thy wyll,
Say well or holde the styll,                              150
For thou haste herde of many a man
A tonge breketh bone and itselfe hath none."

   Than asked ye kynge of ye byrdes by rowe:
"Why cometh not to the parlyament the crowe?
For good counseyll reformeth euery mysse,                 155
And it betokeneth where it is."

   The hawke sayd: "It is no lesse:
Counseyll is good in warre and pese;
But the crowe hath no brayne
For to gyue counseyll but of the rayne."                  160

   Then sayd the hyghwalle with his heed gay:
"He shameth vs with his parlyament araye;
It is a terme with Iohan and Iacke,
'Broken sleue draweth arme abacke.' "

The hawke sayd, "He shall thryue full late          165
That loketh to kepe a grete estate,
And cannot with all his wysdome
Gete hymselfe an hole gowne."

Than sayd the pecoke and the swanne:
"Who no good hath no good canne;          170
And lytell is his wytte sette by
That hathe not to bere out company."

The hawke sayd: "He is worse than wode
That maketh hym fresshe with other mennes good,
Or ought wyll borowe and neuer paye,          175
Or with wronge geteth galaunt araye."

Than in his hole sayd the specke:
"I wolde the hawke brake his necke
Or brought into myscheuous dale,
For of euery byrde he telleth a tale."          180

The hawke sayd: "Thoughe thy castell be in ye tre,
Buylde not aboue thy degre,
For whoso heweth ouer hye,
The chyppes wyll fall in his eye."

Than sayd the kynge: "It is our entente          185
To mende the crowes rayment."
And all the byrdes sayd anone:
"Of eche of our feders he shall haue one."

The hawke sayd: "He may sone come to honeste
That euery man helpeth in his poste,          190
For, as techeth vs the lerned clerke,
Many handes maketh lyght werke."

"I saye," quod the tydyffre, "we Kentysshe men,
We maye not gyue the crowe a pen,
For with them that are sobre and good,          195
A byrde in hande is worthe two in the wood."

The hawke sayd: "I take me to my crede:
Whoso wyll spende with you he maye spede;

Lytell ye gyue, but ye wote why
Ye make the blynde ete many a flye."                          200

    Than ye crowe was put in his araye:
"I am not now as I was yesterdaye;
I am able without offence
To speke in the kynges presence."

    The hawke sayd to the comyns bydene:          205
"Enuye and pryde wolde fayne be sene;
He is worthy none audyence to haue
That cannot say but 'Knaue, knaue.'"

    Than asked the byrdes by aduysement:
"Who is that taketh to vs no tente?                           210
He presumeth before vs all to fle
To the kynges hygh maieste."

    The hawke answered to the whyte semowe:
"He is the sory blacke crowe,
And for hym fareth no man the better:                         215
Lette hym crowe therfore neuer the gretter."

    Than sayd the lordes euerychone:
"We wyll aske of the kynge anone
That euery byrde shall resume
Agayne his fether and his plume,                              220
And make the crowe agayne a knaue,
For he that nought hathe nought shall haue."

    Than sayd the hawke: "As some men sayne
'Borowed ware wyll home agayne.'
And who wyll herken what all men doos                         225
May go helpe to sho the goos."

    For the crowe spake the cormoraunt,
And of his rule made grete auaunt:
"Suche worshyp is reason that euery man haue,
As the kynges hyghnes vouchesaue."                            230

    "Hit is sothe," quod ye hawke, "that thou doost
    say,

Whan all turneth to sporte and playe;
Thou mayst leest speke for the crowes pelfe,
For all thynge loueth that is lyke ytselfe."

  Then prayed the hole parlyamente     235
To the kynge with one assent,
That euery byrde her feder myght
Take frome that proude knyght.

  The kynge sayd: "Ye shall leue haue;
A knyght sholde neuer come of a knaue;    240
All thynge wyll shewe frome whense it come,
Where is his place, and his home."

  "Now trwely;" sayd the hawke then,
"It is grete comforte to all men,
Of the kynges grete prosperyte      245
Whan the kynge ruleth well his comynalte."

  Than was plucked fro the crowe anone
All his feders by one and by one,
And lefte in blacke instede of reed,
And called hym a page of the fyrste heed.   250

  Quod ye hawke: "Ye crowe is now as he shold
   be—
A kynde knaue in his degre;
And he that weneth that no byrde is hym lyke,
Whan his feders are plucked he may hym go pyke."

  Than made the comyns grete noyse,    255
And asked of the lordes with one voyce
That they wolde the hawke exyle
Oute of this londe many a myle,
Neuer to come agayne hyther
But the kynge sende for hym thyder.    260
"Hym to trust we haue no cheson,
For it is preued in truste is treason;
And sythe ye saye he shall not dye
Plucke of his hokes and let hym flye."

  To that sayd the lordes: "We pretende   265

This statute and other to amende,
So in this that ye accorde
To put all in our souerayne lorde."

   The comyns sayd: "It is grete skyll
All thynge to be at the kyngs wyll          270
And vnder the hande of hys grete myght,
By grace his people to seke theyr ryght."

   Than sayde the hawke: "Now to, now fro,
Now labur, now rest, now com, now goo,
Now leeff, now loth, now frynd, now foo:     275
Thus goeth the worlde, in well and wo."

   Than sayd the kynge in his maieste,
"We wyll dyssyuer this grete semble."
He commaunded his chauncelere
The best statutes to rede that he myght here.   280

Thus the fynall iugement
He redde of the byrdes parlyament:
"Wheder they be whyte or blake,
None shall others feders take;
Nor the rauyn plucke the pecockes tayle    285
To make hym fresshe for his auayle;
Nor the comyns feders wante,
For with some they be ryght skante."

   Thus sayeth the cownselle of the iaye,
That none shall vse others araye,         290
For whoso mounteth wyth egle an hye
Shall fayle fethers when he woulde flye.

   Be not gredy glede to gader,
For good fadeth as foules fether;
And though thy fether be not gaye,      295
Haue none enuye at the Swannes aray.

   For thoughe an astryche may eate a nayle,
Wrath wyll plucke his winge and tayle;
And yf thou lye in swalowes nest,
Let not slouth in thy fethers rest.        300

67

Be trewe as turtyll in thy kynde,
For lust wyll part as fethers in wynde;
And he that is a glotonous gull,
Death wyll soone his fethers pull.
Thoughe thou be as hasty as a wype,                    305
And thy fethers flyght-rype,
Loke thy fethers and wrytyng bedene—
What they saye and what they mene.
For here is none other thynge
But fowles, fethers, and wrytyng:                      310
Thus endeth the byrdes parlyment,
By theyr kynges commaundement.

# Textual Notes

## The Harmony of Birds

29. Without]   W hout   *(edge of page imperfect)*
*51. fath]   W bath
70. *Et*]   W t   } *(edge of page imperfect)*
*71. *Sot*]   W ot
83. *Incessabile*]   W in cessabile
112. Than]   W han   } *(edge of page imperfect)*
113. *Te*]   W e
150. laude]   W luade
153. *aura*]   W aure
154. *Patrem*]   W atrem   }
155. That]   W hat   } *(edge of page imperfect)*
166. reherse]   W rehers   }
183. *vox*]   W vos
197. Without]   W witout
213. reuyue]   W reuyu   *(edge of page imperfect)*
256. *homine*]   W omni
261. tower]   W towe   *(edge of page imperfect)*
269. *passeribus*]   W pastoribus
303. *Miserere*]   W misere
330. *confundar*]   W confunder

## The Parliament of Birds

A. READINGS REJECTED FROM BASE TEXT

17. he (LV)]   K be
19. saw (LV)]   K same
26. fle (L)]   KV flye
32. soth (LV)]   K so
44. to (KLV)]   W *omits*

48. mewe (KLV)]   W . . we *(partially obliterated)*
49. alone (KLV)]   W a one (l *possibly obliterated)*
65. whoso (KLV)]   W how so
68. ye (KV)]   W or   L and
71. Than (KLV)]   W thon
72. sayde (KV)]   W saythe   L *omits*
*74. hem]   WKLV hym
76. ought (KLV)]   W nought
*87. blustred]   W blussed   KV blushed   L bloshed
90. mere (L)]   WKV myre
91. want (KLV)]   W wanton
93. this done ys]   WKV this done was   L ys done
*110. Meueth]   WKLV meneth
112. nowght (L)]   WKV not
118. londe (L)]   W lounde   KV lande
119. chyyde (KV)]   WL chyde
130. wyll (KLV)]   W was
      leaue alyue (KV)]   W destroyed   L dystroy
131. For nere (L)]   WKV in
133. he plucketh (KLV)]   W plucked
135. We thynke (KLV)]   W unthynketh
*138. fordone]   WKLV forgone
142. kepe (KLV)]   W kepeth
153. asked (L)]   WKV answered
      rowe (KLV)]   W rewe
157. hawke (KLV)]   W hawek
161. hyghwalle (L)]   WKV nyghtwhale (W hyghwall MS
      *handwritten in margin)*
195. are (KV)]   W are not   L be not
213. semowe (L)]   WKV semewe
227. the[1] (KLV)]   W to
231. quod]   W quud   L quoth   KV sayd
234. ytselfe (KLV)]   W hymselfe
263. not (KLV)]   W *repeats*
264. his (KV)]   WL this
270. thynge (KLV)]   W thyne
272. theyr (KLV)]   W his
274–75. Now . . . foo (L)]   WKV *omit*
287. Nor (L)]   WKV for
289. cownselle (L)]   K chosen   V cosen
294. as (L)]   KV and
297. a (LV)]   K *omits*
306. thy (LV)]   K the

B. OTHER SUBSTANTIVE VARIANTS

1. is]   L *omits*
2. For]   L of
3. it]   L *omits*
5. noyse]   L morinne
   on]   L in
   syde]   L sted
6. so . . . pride]   L of
   fowle and byrd
7. Therfore]   L wherfor
   in bylles]   L ther byllys
   in
8. theyr]   L your
9. in]   L and hys
10. sette in]   L made
    lawful]   VL lefull
11. great]   L *omits*
13. thyne and myne]   L
    myn and thyne
14. great and small]   L
    smale and grett
    estate]   L state
15. synge sayd]   L songe
    quoth
16. weake . . . euer]   L
    wekest alway takyth
18. as]   L be yt
    is]   L or
20. and]   L *omits*
22. song]   L *adds* a seson
25. diuers . . . be]   L and
    dyuers bee
26. no]   L *omits*
    nor]   V ne
29. it]   L *omits*
    to]   L *omits*
32. sayth]   L *adds* the
    soth]   L *adds* he
33. maye . . . of]   L now
    may say the
38. to]   L *omits*
42. are]   L *omits*
45. that]   L *omits*
46. leest]   L lest
    may]   KV *add* he

47. they]   K al the byrdes
    V *omits*
51. Ye fayle]   KV *repeat*
52. not]   KV no
53. but]   L *omits*
54. They shall]   L nor they
    shulde
    as they]   L at your
55. Anone than]   L then
    anon
    sange]   V synge
57. The]   KV that
    can well]   L wyll can
61. songe]   KLV synge
63. rombled]   L rombyd
66. mery]   L merth
68. or]   L *omits*
69. ne]   KL nor
71. the$^1$ . . . wode]   L in the
    wood the fesaunde
72. men]   V med
    he]   L *omits*
    good]   L lande
73. ne$^1$]   KLV nor
    ne$^2$]   KV nor
    food]   L goode
74. It fleteth]   L alle fleyth
77. the]   KLV *omit*
81. wysteleth]   L whistylle
83. sayd]   L quoth
    by]   K buy
84. Saye]   L sye
    whan]   KV for
88. dobchyk]   K bobchick
89. The]   L that
90. he]   K be
91. want]   L *adds* your
94. lyue]   L leue
95. creked]   L *repeats*
98. charge]   L barge
102. faste]   KV *omit*
103. creked]   K creeped
104. make]   L makyth
    lame]   L to wane
105. that]   L *omits*
106. ouerblowe]   L blow

107. can]　L wylle
109. haue]　KLV hath
111. The]　L then the
112. may nowght]　L
　　　nowght may
112, 114. auayle]　L vaylle
116. his]　K *omits*
118. thynge]　KV *omit*
120. bereth]　KV beare
121. aryse]　L ryse
122. themselfe]　L them-
　　　selvys
　　　on]　KV in
123. his]　L thys
125. lyue]　L leve
128. some]　L *adds* men
129. ne[1,2]]　K nor　L and
130. may]　KV myght
132. In]　L in the
133. a]　L *omits*
134. full]　L *omits*
135. the]　KV by
140. hymselfe]　L them-
　　　selvyn
141. dystresse]　L dystresses
142. gesse]　L chesses
143. not]　L *omits*
144. But]　K except
　　　L tylle
145. sayd]　L spak
146. Lytell]　L and sayd
　　　lytylle
147. elles]　L *omits*
　　　ne]　K nor
148. bet[1]]　L bytt
149. quod]　L sayd
　　　wyll]　L bylle
151. For]　KV *omit*
152. A]　L *omits*
　　　itselfe]　L selfe
153. of]　KV and
　　　by]　K a
154. cometh]　L com
155. mysse]　L messe
156. betokeneth]　L be takyn
157. no]　KV not

73

158. and] L *adds* in
160. For] L *omits*
     gyue] L *adds* any
161. sayd] L spake
     gay] L gray
162. vs] L *omits*
163. is] L *omits*
164. Broken] V broked
     sleue] L shyn
165. The . . . sayd] L quoth
       the hawk
167. wysdome] L wydom
       preve
168. Gete] L to gett
     gowne] L sleve
176. geteth galaunt] L
       getyth hym galaundes
177. his] L her
     sayd] L spake
     specke] L wood spok
178. brake] L had broke
     his] L her
179. into] KV vnto some
180. telleth] L makyth
184. chyppes] L chyp
     fall] L *adds* down
186. mende] KL amende
       V amande
     rayment] L arayment
187. sayd] L say
188. eche] L ylke
     he] K be
189. The . . . sayd] L quoth
       the hawk
190. in] L after
     poste] L postee
192. maketh] L make
193. I saye] L syth
     quod] KV sayd
     tydyffre] L tedyffe
     we] L with the
     Kentysshe] L Norfolk
195. sobre] L saber
198. with] V wit *(capitalized)*
     he] L *omits*
199. wote] L wyt

202. I am]   L yt ys
     as I was]   L quoth he
203. am]   L *adds* now
205. hawke]   L hak
207. is]   L *adds* not
209. by]   L with
210. is]   L *adds* thys
212. To]   L yevyn to
213. to]   L *omits*
214. He]   KLV it
215. fareth no man]   L no
       man faryth
216. crowe . . . the]   L neuer
       grow to
218. aske . . . kynge]   L of
       the kyng aske
     anone]   KV abone
220. fether]   L fedures
222. he that]   L who
223. men]   KV *omit*
224. ware]   L good
225. who]   L whos
     herkon]   L smattur
     all men]   KV euery
       man
232. all]   L *adds* thyng
233. mayst]   L mast
     leest]   L lest
238. frome]   L *adds* the crow
241. shewe]   L keth
     whense]   L when
242. his]   L *adds* owyn
243. sayd]   L quoth
244. is]   KV *add* a
245. grete]   L good
246. the . . . ruleth]   L he
       rewlys
249. in]   KV all
     instede]   L in the stede
250. hym]   L *omits*
251. Ye crowe]   L *omits*
     is now]   L now ys he
253. that²]   KLV *omit*
     byrde . . . lyke]   L
       byrdes lyke hym

75

254. hym go pyke]   L go
         pyke hym
258. this]   L the
260. for]   K to
261. cheson]   KV theson
263. sythe]   L sens
264. hokes]   L lokkys
265. sayd]   L quoth
         pretende]   L condes-
         cende
266. This statute]   L theys
         fawtys
268. in]   K to
271. hande]   L hawk
272. his]   KV the
276. the]   L thys
         well]   L wele
277. in]   L of
         his]   L adds hye
280. best]   L omits
         he]   L they
281. Thus]   L thys ys
282. redde]   L radde
283. Wheder]   L that wether
285. rauyn]   L adds to
290. araye]   V ary
291. mounteth]   L mount
         wyth]   L adds the
         an]   L to
292. woulde]   L shold
293. not]   L no
         glede]   L adds goodes
294. fadeth]   L wylle melt
295. thy fether]   L the blake
         fetherys
296. the]   L omits
298. his]   LV him
299. lye]   L logge
300. thy]   L omits
305. as¹]   L omits
         a]   L the
306. flyght-rype]   V slyght
         rype
309. here is]   L yett is herre
311. endeth]   L fenyshth

# Commentary

EACH REFERENCE TO A BOOK OR ARTICLE NOT INCLUDED IN the table of Abbreviations is followed by an indication of the section of the Bibliography in which it is listed.

## The Harmony of Birds

1–24.    The first four stanzas set the scene in a manner reminiscent of the *chansons d'aventure*: see Introduction, pp. 31–32.

2.    "At the break of day." This line was probably composed by the poet himself, in contrast to most of the Latin lines in the poem.

25.    *popyngay*: "parrot." Contemporary usage of "popinjay" and "parrot" seems to have been more or less indiscriminate: Turner employs both words to translate Lat. *psittacus* (pp. 150/ 51, 208/09), and both occur in Skelton's *SP.*

27.    "This he learned through me." Source unlocated; a variation on the scripturally-based line 30.

30.    "Learn always from me." An echo of *discite a me* (Matt. 11:29).

34–35.    The parrot similarly initiates the praise of God in *The Birds' Devotions*, 22–35.

36.    *Te Deum Laudamus:* The opening of the *TD.* With this quotation the poet begins his schematic interweaving of lines from the *TD* into his poem. See Introduction, p. 31.

37.    *auys:* "bird." The Latin word is no doubt used in order to provide a rhyme for *mavys* in the following line.

38.    *mauys:* Two types of thrush are mentioned in the poem: the *mauys* or "song thrush" (elsewhere also termed the *throstle*), and the *thrusshe* or "mistle thrush" (*HB* 85). The distinction between

the two birds is specified by Turner (pp. 170/71–72/73), and is reflected (e.g.) in Skelton, *PS,* 424–25 and 460.

39–47.    The song thrush is commonly praised for its beautiful voice (as in *The Birds' Praise of Love,* 25–32): thus its association here with the technical aspects of singing has a certain aptness.

39.    *ellamy:* The *OED* glosses *e-la-mi:* "The note E, sung to the syllable *la* or *mi* according as it occurred in one or other of the Hexachords to which it belonged."

41.    *round:* "mellow." Though the earliest usage of the word in this sense recorded by the *OED* is dated 1832, the context would seem to make it clear that this is what the poet intends.

45.    The birds are imagined performing a harmonized arrangement.

48.    The second half of *TD* 1.

49.    *partryge:* There is no sign here of the various, but usually negative, associations of the partridge in bird lore: see de Thaun, pp. 108–09; McCulloch, pp. 152–53; Rowland, pp. 123–27; Swainson, p. 173.

51.    *fath:* W reads *bath,* which clearly makes very poor sense. Of the words which would rhyme with *path* (54), *fath*—a form of "faith" found mainly in fifteenth–century texts—seems the most acceptable. It would not be without parallel for the poet to employ an unusual form for the sake of the rhyme: cf. *wunt* ("wont"), used in line 97 to rhyme with *sunt; sun* ("son," line 190, with *run*), and *quere* ("quire," line 293, with *here*).

59–60.    *TD* 2, complete.

63–64.    The peacock's discordant voice is regularly commented upon by writers on bird lore: according to Bartholomaeus, he "haþ an horrible voys" (12:32). Thus *brest* is no doubt used in the (relatively uncommon) sense "voice in singing" (*OED,* sense 6).

66.    Chaucer terms them "aungel fethres bright" (Chaucer, *PF,* 356). In medieval paintings, angels were often depicted with peacock feathers in their wings: see Giffin, 1956 (III.B), pp. 49–66. Thus the attribution of lines 67–70 to the peacock is particularly appropriate.

67–70.    The Latin words make up the text of *TD* 3, less the final word *potestates*—which is presumably rendered by *estates* in line 71.

71.    *Sot:* The emendation is conjectural, but represents the most acceptable means of completing the textual reading *-ot.*

73–84.    The nightingale is, of course, more usually identified with passionate human love than with divine love. Nevertheless, the latter association—as here in *HB*—is well attested: see Lampe, 1967 (II.B), pp. 55–56. The rich and complex range of ideas, stories, and associations which grew up around the nightingale between the classical period and the Renaissance are considered by: Chandler, 1934 and 1938; Raby, 1951; Shippey, 1970; and Telfer, 1952 (all III.B). See also Rowland, pp. 105–111; Swainson, pp. 18–22; and Swann, pp. 166–67, 178.

79–80, 83–84.   *TD* 4, complete.

85.   *thrusshe:* See *HB* n.38, above.

86–87, 89–90.   *TD* 5, complete. *Sabaoth* is the Hebrew for "hosts."

91–96.   Detailed accounts of the traditions associated with the lark are provided by Bawcutt, 1972, and Chandler, 1938 (both III.B). See also Rowland, pp. 97–101; and Swainson, p. 94.

97.   *wunt:* "wont." On the unusual spelling, see n.51 above. In the *OED*, *wunt* is acknowledged as a form of the verb *want*, but not of the substantive.

98–99, 102.   *TD* 6, complete.

103–14.   The cock's ability to tell the time is frequently mentioned by writers from Pliny (Pliny, *NH,* 10:21) on. Allusion to the idea occurs, for instance, in Chaucer's *Nun's Priest's Tale* (Chaucer, *CT,* 7:2850–58) and Skelton, *PS,* 495–512; see also White, p. 151; McCulloch, p. 104. Poets and commentators often praise the cock for his effectiveness in calling people to worship and in waking them from spiritual slumber—ideas reflected, no doubt, in lines 106–7. Views of the cock in classical and Christian tradition are discussed by Allen, 1954 (III.B). See also Knortz, pp. 179–214; and Rowland, pp. 20–28.

106.   *postle:* An aphetic form of "apostle."

111.   "At his touch brought forth the company" (i.e., the company of apostles: see line 114).

113–14.   *TD* 7, complete.

115–20.   According to Maplet, the magpie "had his Latin name first of Pycus Saturnes sonne which in his prophesying and soothsaying vsed this birde" (p. 167). Though associated with prophecy and augury in general, he is often regarded specifically as a bird of ill omen: see Hare, pp. 41–42; Rowland, p. 104; Swainson, pp. 76–81; and Swann, pp. 151–52. The poem here modifies this aspect of the traditional associations of the magpie in order to present him in a more dignified and positive light—praising his skill in prophecy and actually identifying him with the Christian prophets (lines 116, 119).

118.   This is a quotation from Ps. 17:8: *Sub umbra alarum tuarum protege me.* Its relevance to this context seems marginal—though Psalm 17 is used in the compline service.

119–20.   *TD* 8, complete.

121–32.   The point is that the domestic birds are killed in order to feed man: thus the poet makes the (somewhat strained) connection between their self-sacrifice and that of the Christian martyrs.

127, 130, 132.   *TD* 9, complete.

133–38.   Instances of robins actually living in churches are recorded by Lack (pp. 5–7, 107–08). These lines may also reflect less specifically various legends in which the robin does good or holy deeds (see, e.g., Lack, pp. 29–57, 90–93; Swainson, pp. 15–18; and Swann, pp. 198–99). Compare the role accorded him in Skelton's *PS:* "And Robyn Redbrest, / He shall be the preest, / The Requiem masse to synge, / Softly warbelynge" (399–402). Traditions associated with the robin are reviewed in Rowland, pp. 149–54. See also note to *HB* 187–92, below.

139, 142, 144.   *TD* 10, complete.

140.   "According to the use of Salisbury." In the early to mid sixteenth century, three "uses" were employed: York in the north, Hereford in a small area of the Welsh border country, and Salisbury in the rest of England (see Wordsworth and Littlehales, 1904 [IV.B], pp. 5–8).

141.   *cum gloria:* "with glory." The words *cum gloria* occur in a number of texts in the Vulgate, but it seems unlikely that the poet means this to be understood as a specific quotation. He may, perhaps, intend an allusion to the *Gloria in excelsis.* This, like the *TD,* is a hymn in praise of God, and its theme and tone are thus in keeping with *HB* (though, whereas the *TD* is performed during matins, the *Gloria* forms part of the mass). On the *Gloria,* see Podhradsky, 1967 (IV.B), pp. 95–96.

145–50.   In bird lore the eagle is often, but not invariably, represented as king of the birds: see Armstrong, pp. 145–50. References to the royalty of the eagle are common in literature: see, for instance, Chaucer, *PF,* 330; Lydgate, *Cok,* 41; Dunbar, *Thistle,* 120; *PB* 8 and passim.

151–52   The eagle's ability to look straight at the sun is a commonplace of bird lore (see, e.g., Bartholomaeus, 12:2; McCulloch, p. 114; Armstrong, pp. 134–35; Swainson, p. 134; and Swann, p. 98). This idea is frequently alluded to in literature: see, e.g., Dante, *Paradiso,* 1:43–54; Chaucer, *PF,* 331. However, it is possible (particularly in view of the conjunction with the phoenix in 151ff.) that the poet is here referring to another tradition: that the aged eagle, having grown feeble and dim-sighted, flies to the sun, which burns away his old feathers and the mist obscuring his eyes, then plunges three times into a spring, and is thus rejuvenated. Allusion to this idea may be found, for instance, in: Ps. 103:5 (also cf. Exod. 19:4, Isa. 40:31); White, p. 105; McCulloch, pp. 113–14; and Bartholomaeus, 12:2. See also Robin, pp. 160–62; Rowland, pp. 51–53; and Swainson, p. 134.

153.  "His eyes scourged by the brilliance." A minor emendation is necessary, since W *aure* is syntactically incorrect.

154, 156.  *TD* 11, complete.

157–62.  Surveys of the legends associated with the phoenix may be found in Robin, pp. 36–43, and Rowland, pp. 134–40. The uniqueness of the phoenix is regularly emphasized by the authors of encyclopedias and bestiaries: see (e.g.) Pliny, *NH*, 10:2; de Thaun, p. 115; McCulloch, p. 158; and Bartholomaeus, 12:15. This notion is reflected in many works of literature, for instance, the ME poem *Pearl*, 429–32; Chaucer, *Book of the Duchess*, 982; Skelton, *PS*, 516–17. The central and essential story about the phoenix is, of course, that of its burning and rebirth. As a consequence, it came to symbolize resurrection, and this association in turn led to its identification with Christ—as, for example, in the bestiaries (see McCulloch, p. 158).

163–68.  The speaker of this verse could be either the phoenix or the poet. In view of the fact that the poet does not elsewhere interrupt the birds' statements of praise, it seems likely that the former is the case, and the lines have been punctuated accordingly.

165, 168.  The poet omits the word *tuum* from the text of *TD* 12, on which these lines are based.

169–74.  The allusion occurs in all four Gospels: see Matt. 3:16, Mark 1:10, Luke 3:22, John 1:32. Some of the bestiaries also reflect this identification between the Holy Ghost and the dove: see de Thaun, pp. 116–18; and McCulloch, p. 111.

179–80.  *TD* 13, complete.

183.  "All in one voice." The poet is apparently translating line 181. A minor emendation is necessary in order to make sense of the Latin.

185.  "From 'do' to 're'." These notes are equivalent respectively to C and D in the natural scale of C major.

186.  *TD* 14, with the initial *Et* added by the poet.

187–92.  This well-known connection is encapsulated in the popular rhyme: "The robin redbreast and the wren / Are God

Almighty's cock and hen." It is alluded to (e.g.) by Skelton, *PS*, 600–601, and Drayton, *The Owl*, 698. See also Swainson, pp. 18, 35; Swann, p. 261; and Hare, p. 33.

190. *Sun:* "Son." The spelling reflects the rhyme with *run:* cf. n.51, above.

196, 198. *TD* 15, complete.

199. *tyrtle trew:* The truth of the turtle dove is one of the most frequently repeated commonplaces of bird lore; allusions to it may be found in all kinds of literature. Maplet explains the idea as follows: ". . . hir best praise is in keeping vndefiled wedlock and (lesing hir Mate) for hir constant widowhoode" (p. 176). See also (e.g.) McCulloch, p. 178; Chaucer, *PF*, 355, 577, 582–88; *The Birds' Praise of Love*, 13; *The Court of Love*, 234, 1395; and Skelton, *PS*, 465. Cf. *PB* 301.

202–04. The turtle dove is also associated with the Virgin Mary in de Thaun, p. 119.

205–10. An adroit and contextually apposite reworking of *TD* 16. Lines 205–07 may be rendered: "Thou in order to deliver and save condemned man . . ."; line 209: "but chose."

211–16. According to the traditional story, the pelican chicks strike their parents who in return strike and kill them; after three days, the mother pierces her breast and revives the dead chicks with her blood. Thus the pelican was taken to symbolize Christ. This story is one of the best-known in the whole of bird lore, appearing (for instance) in: de Thaun, pp. 115–16; White, pp. 132–33; Bartholomaeus, 12:30; Turner, pp. 152/53; and Maplet, pp. 165–66; see also McCulloch, pp. 155–57; Rowland, pp. 130–33; Swann, pp. 155–56; Hare, p. 101; and Robin, pp. 65–68. It is frequently alluded to in literature, as, for instance, in Dante's *Paradiso* (25:113), where Christ is termed "our pelican," and in *The Birds' Devotions* 36–42, where the symbol of the pelican is identified with Christ's passion. "The pelican in her piety" is a familiar illustration in the bestiaries (see, e.g., White, p. 132; McCulloch, plate 7, fig. 4; and Millar, 1958 [III.A], plate 58); it also appears as a heraldic device (see Vinycomb, 1906 [III.B], pp. 182–86). The legend may well be based on (slightly misinterpreted) observation of the pelican's habits in feeding her young (see Martin, p. 158). The entire tradition is reviewed in Graham, 1962 (III.B).

217–18. The first part of *TD* 17.

219–20. "Thou has ascended as the Lord of Lords." These lines are interpolated by the poet into the text of *TD* 17, quoted in lines 217–18 and 21–22. He probably assembled them himself;

*Dominus dominorum* is, however, a stock formula, and *Tu ascen-disti* is a quotation from Ps. 68:18.

221–22.   The second part of *TD* 17, with the addition of *Et* at the beginning of line 221.

223–28.   The metaphor in these lines is based on the device of visualizing the blackbird's song in the form of musical notes written down ("pricked") in the traditional black and red ink. In the second part of the stanza—punning on *pricke* in the sense of "pierce," and drawing on the similarity in appearance between the red notes and drops of blood—the poet connects the song with the image of Christ's passion and crown of thorns.

231.   "On the right hand of Majesty"—i.e., of God. This is probably a line of the poet's own, inserted to fulfill the require-ments of the stanza and functioning as a kind of variation on *TD* 18 (see below, lines 233–34).

233–34.   *TD* 18, complete.

236–37.   Writers on bird lore usually state that swallows build their nests on men's houses, sometimes adding that they em-ploy similar principles of construction: see (e.g.) White, pp. 147–48; McCulloch, p. 175; Turner, pp. 96/97; and cf. Ps. 84:3. Bar-tholomaeus suggests that swallows "loueþ mannes companye" (12:22). There is also a popular belief that it is lucky to have a swallow build under one's eaves (see Hare, pp. 21–22; and Arm-strong, pp. 181–82), perhaps related to the notion that swallows are endowed with foreknowledge and will desert a building which is going to collapse (see McCulloch, p. 175).

241.   The poet is probably alluding to the swallow's migratory habits, known to most medieval writers on bird lore (see, e.g., White, p. 147; McCulloch, p. 175; and Bartholomaeus, 12:22), though some later writers, including Turner (pp. 96/97) repeat the false notion that the swallow hibernates during the winter: see *PB* 299–300 and note.

245–46.   *TD* 19, complete.

253, 255.   The first part of *TD* 20. The Latin more usually reads *famulis tuis.*

256.   *Ab homine doloso:* The emendation (of W *omni* to *homine*) is necessary, since the poet is evidently quoting from Ps. 43:1 *(ab homine iniquo et doloso erue me).* Psalm 43 is used at the beginning of the Tridentine Mass.

257–58.   The second part of *TD* 20.

259–64.   This positive view of the hawks is in complete contrast to the treatment in *PB*, where their role is subjected to a sus-tained, if somewhat ambivalent, critical scrutiny.

260.   *belles:* See *PB,* n.83 below. Again, the contrast with *PB* is striking, for here the ringing of the bells is used to associate the hawks with worship. But even this association was employed in contemporary literature to make a critical point. In Skelton's *Ware the Hawk,* the hawk's bells are ironically equated with church bells (lines 124, 136–37) in order to suggest that the wicked priest values secular sport more highly than his pastoral duties.

261.   *tower:* Though the meaning might at first appear simply to be "tower," it is more likely that the poet intended "lofty flight," or perhaps wordplay between the two senses. The word *tower* (noun and verb) was used as a technical term to describe the circular flight of a soaring hawk. It is ultimately derived from OF *tour* ("turn, wheel"), but was assimilated into the English "tower" (OE *tur*): thus the two senses possible here are fundamental to its development. (See *OED,* s.v. *tower,* sb.¹, sense 8, and *tour,* sb.; and Hands's note, pp. 104–05, to the phrase *hawkes of the towre.*

268–70.   Probably "As His [Christ's] heirs, you are of greater value than many sparrows." No source for the first part of this line has been found, and it is almost certainly by the poet. The second and third lines represent a slightly modified version of Luke 12:7: *multis passeribus pluris estis vos.* It is hardly necessary to defend the emendation of *pastoribus* to *passeribus.* These lines do, however, raise an issue of more substantial interest, in that they contain the poet's single major departure from his otherwise virtually complete consistency in the use of the text of the *TD.* One would expect him to quote here from *TD* 21 but this is the only verse of *TD* from which he makes no quotation. These lines (*HB* 268–70) are thus substitutes for *TD* 21—though there is no obvious connection between the two texts and no apparent reason for the substitution.

272–73, 275–76.   *TD* 22, complete.

279.   "That they may not fall into hell": probably a line of the poet's own.

280–82.   *TD* 23, complete.

286.   The opening of the Lord's Prayer in Latin. See Matt. 6:9–13.

287–88.   *TD* 24, complete.

289–94.   With the exception of *Et gloriosus* (syntactically very awkward, but perhaps best translated, "and full of glory,") the Latin follows the text of *TD* 25. *Et gloriosus* forms part of the fourth responsory at the end of the *TD* as traditionally used in the church: it reads in full: *Et laudabilis, et gloriosus at superexaltatus in saecula.*

297. *exire:* "depart."

298–300. *TD* 26, complete.

303, 306. These lines are made up from *TD* 27.

311–12. The first part of *TD* 28.

317–18. The second part of *TD* 28.

325–26. The poet adds *cotidie* ("daily") to the first part of *TD* 29.

327. "Into hell."

330. The second part of *TD* 29. The erroneous form *confunder* in W has been emended to *confundar.*


## The Parliament of Birds

7. The variant reading in L suggests that the scribe understood *bylles* in its alternative sense of "petitions" (as opposed to "beaks").

8. *kyng:* See note to *HB* 145–50.

11. *grype:* This probably means "vulture," though the word could also be used to mean "griffin." Lines 12–14 reflect the views of vultures found both in bird lore and in literature: their greed (as in "gredy grypes": Skelton, *PS*, 307) or their habit of feeding on dead carcasses (as in Maplet, p. 178).

12. *Owne is owne:* Tilley, O.100; Whiting, O.76. That is, "what is one's own is one's own"—the sinister implication of which is specified in the following half line: "whoever can take it." Thus the line as a whole suggests the traditional view of the vulture's greedy and rapacious character.

15. Cf. Whiting, C.600: "The cuckoo can sing but one lay (song)"; Tilley, C.894: "You are like the cuckoo, you have but one song"; and Lydgate's *Churl:* "The cokkow syngen can but o lay" (line 346: Lydgate, *MP,* 2:483). Topsell observes that "the voice of this birde is *Coco,* without alteration, and the often reiteration thereof breedeth no delight in the hearer" (p. 239). Unflattering judgements of the cuckoo's song are common in the literature of the Renaissance. Cf. *PB* 21–22 and note.

16. These sentiments are expressed in a number of proverbs: cf. Tilley, W.183–85; Whiting, W.128–31. The cuckoo's nesting habits were the subject of comment from Pliny (*NH,* 10:11) on. Thus, in Chaucer's *PF,* the cuckoo is termed "ever unkynde" (358), and is addressed as "Thow mortherere of the hyesoge

[hedge sparrow] on the braunche / That broughte the forth"
(612–13).

17–18.   Cf. Whiting, M.534: "Might is (overcomes) right
*(varied)*"; Tilley, M.922: "Might overcomes right."

21–22.   Cf. "to sing the same (one) song" (Tilley, S.638; Whiting, S.479), and *PB* n.15.

23.   Perhaps a jesting reference to the fictional device, essential
to the fable and related forms, of granting the power of speech
to birds (or beasts). Cf. Chaucer, *Nun's Priest's Tale, CT,* 7:2880–
81.

25.   *diuers:* The term *hawk* is unspecific (like Lat. *accipiter*), and
the birds are here perhaps referring to the divers varieties covered by the general term, though no further differentiation between the various types occurs in the poem. In hawking manuals, on the other hand, it is common to find not only discussion
of the differing qualities of the various species, but also lists
stating which bird of prey is appropriate to men of each particular social class (see Hands, pp. 54–55; Phipson, pp. 245–49).

26.   *fle:* The emendation is justified by the stronger sense of
"flee" as opposed to "fly," and is supported by the rhyme. Elsewhere in the text there is some confusion between the forms *fle*
and *flye* in the sense "fly": see n.96, below.

27.   *prating pye:* References to the magpie's delight in chattering
are common from Pliny onward (see Pliny, *NH* 10:43, repeated
in Turner, pp. 142/43) and alluded to in the bestiaries (see
McCulloch, pp. 141–42; White, p. 138), in various works of literature (e.g., Chaucer, *PF,* 345; Skelton, *PS,* 397), and in the folk
name, "chatterpie" (see Swainson, p. 76; cf. Swann, p. 158). Cf.
*HB* 115–20 and note.

28.   Tilley, W.828. Cf. Whiting, W.593: "In fele [i.e., many] lies
*(varied)*"—examples of which include Lydgate, *Churl,* 200.

32.   Whiting, S.492—examples of which include Lydgate, *Cok,*
135. Cf. Tilley T.569: "Truth begets hatred."

36.   Whiting, S.485. Cf. Tilley, T.594: "All truths must not be
told."

39.   *popyngeiay:* See *HB* n.25.

*paradyse:* The association of the parrot with paradise is common
in the poetry of the late Middle Ages and Renaissance. Thus, in
Lydgate's *Cok* we find "Popyngayes froo Paradys comyn al
grene" (91), while Skelton's *SP* opens, "My name ys Parott, a
byrde of Paradyse," and includes a further reference to this connection (in lines 186–87). See Fisher, 1945 (III.B).

40.   Cf. Whiting, W.379: "It is great wisdom to speak little"; S.585: "Whoso speaks unwisely speaks too much."

41–42.   Tilley cites this as a variant of L.358: "Little (nothing) said, soon amended." The parrot also comments on the spending of money in Skelton, *SP,* lines 335 and 460–61.

48.   *mewe:* This word originally existed as a substantive meaning the place in which a hawk was shut away in order to moult and a verb signifying this process.

53.   *Comyns:* "the common people," but perhaps also suggesting "the House of Commons," with reference to the poem's extended parliamentary metaphor (see *PB* 109, 121, 127; and Introduction, pp. 35–36).

56.   *notes many:* Pliny commends the copiousness of the nightingale's song in *NH,* 10:43.

58.   Maplet observes that "many Caesars or Emperours . . . haue had Nightingales" (p. 159).

63.   *for her lot:* i.e., of not having a good voice.

63–66.   Bartholomaeus (in Trevisa's translation) says of the dove that she "haþ gronynge in stede of song" (12:7).

70.   This may be intended as a reference to the fate of Lambert Simnel, *qui postea deuicto Ioanne Comite Lincolniense, eius ductore, in coquina regia diu uoluit ueru, ac deinde accipitrum domitor est factus* ("who afterwards, when his mentor John earl of Lincoln was defeated, became a turnspit in the royal kitchen before he was promoted to be the trainer of the royal hawks"): *The Anglica Historia of Polydore Vergil, A.A. 1485–1537,* ed. and trans. Denys Hay (London: Camden Society, 1950), Book 24, pp. 70/71.

74.   Cf. Whiting, W.148: "Wealth ebbs and flows as the flood." *hem:* Though all texts read *hym,* the emendation may be justified by the need to agree with the plural *men* in line 72.

77.   *foly:* Nearer *OED,* sense 2 (s.v. *folly*), "wickedness, evil, mischief, harm," than "folly," which seems inappropriate.

80.   *out of nocke:* A metaphor from archery: the original meaning of *nock* was "one of the small tips of horn fixed at each end of a bow and provided with a notch for holding the string" *(OED).*

81.   *osyll . . . byrdes blake:* Contemporary writers on birds regarded the terms *ouzel* (spelled variously) and *blackbird* as synonymous. Turner glosses Lat. *merula,* "a blak osel, a blak byrd" (pp. 114/15); Topsell's account of this bird is headed, "The Blackbird or Owsell or Blackmacke" (p. 93). Thus *byrdes blake* seems a little odd—it repeats what has already been said, and its plural is awkward. It is best taken as a general and unspecific reference

to (? other) black birds rather than a specific reference to black-birds. Cf. *HB* 223.

*wysteleth:* Cf. Whiting, O.57: "As the ouzel whistles so answers the thrush."

82.   Cf. Tilley, A.35: "Make ado and have ado."

83.   *belles:* These were fixed to hawks' legs in order to help falconers locate them and are described in *The Boke of St. Albans* (Hands, p. 53; see also Hands's notes on these lines, p. 105). An illustration of a hawk's bell is provided by Harting, 1871 (III.B), p. 60.

87.   *blustred:* The textual readings (W *blussed,* KV *blushed,* L *bloshed*) can represent only the past tense of *blush,* which offers no acceptable sense (see *OED,* s.v. *blush*). In view of the pattern established in the preceding stanzas, one would expect here a verb indicating either the act of speaking (as in *sayd* [75, 83], *spake* [39], and *bade* [43]) or else a bird sound (as in *sange* [55], *rombled* [63], and *crowed* [71, 79]). The emendation restores this pattern as well as the sense, *blustred* being understood as an elided form of *blustered,* "blasted, uttered a blasting sound" (see next note).

*bottore:* This name is more commonly spelled with an *i* (or a *y,* as in KV *byttur*), but the form with *o* is attested elsewhere. The bittern's main claim to celebrity was its cry. Ornithologists and poets alike exercised considerable ingenuity in their attempts to describe the production and nature of this remarkable sound. Turner writes: *ad ripas lacuum et paludium desidet, ubi rostrum in aquas inserens, tantos edit bombos, ut ad miliarium Italicum facile possit audiri* ("it sits about the sides of lakes and marshes, where putting its beak into the water it gives utterance to such a booming as may easily be heard an Italian mile away"): pp. 124/5–26/7. Topsell quotes *inque paludiferis Butio butit aquis* from an unknown source, adding the delightful translation, "And in fenne waters not in rockes / The Bittour roareth like an Oxe" (p. 88). Chaucer mentions how "a bitore bombleth in the myre" (*Wife of Bath's Tale, CT,* 3:972), Skelton refers to "The bitter with his bumpe" (*PS,* 432), while Drayton offers a more elaborate description: "The Buzzing *Bitter* sits, which through his hollow Bill, / A sudden bellowing sends, which many times doth fill / The neighbouring *Marsh* with noyse, as though a Bull did roare" (*Poly-Olbion,* song 25, 103–05). See also Martin, pp. 46–47; and Rowland, pp. 9–10.

90.   *sowsed:* "plunged." The verb *souse* is also used in the language of falconry to mean "swoop." The poet may have intended an entirely appropriate and rather witty play on the two

senses of the word—but the earliest *OED* citation of *souse* in the latter sense is dated 1589.

*mere:* The emendation is supported by the rhyme. It is possible that the appearance of *myre* in three texts out of four is explained by the familiarity of the phrase, "in the mire," accorded proverbial status by both Tilley (M.989) and Whiting (M.573).

91.   *Wysshers want wyll:* Cf. Whiting, W.402: "One may not have by wishes"; and Tilley, W.535–38.

96.   *fle:* W normally has *fle* for "fly"—in contrast to the other three texts, which usually have *flye.* The *OED* regards *fle* in this sense as a legitimate spelling during the sixteenth century, and thus there is no ground for emendation. Indeed, the use of *fle* to rhyme with *maieste* (lines 211–12) and of *flye* to rhyme with *dye* and *hye* (lines 263–64, 291–92) indicates that the poet was willing to use both forms. For comment on the confusion between "fly" and "flee," see *OED*, s.v. *flee.*

98.   The sense of the line depends on the interpretation of *charge.* Perhaps the least inappropriate definition is "duty or responsibility of taking care of someone; custody" (*OED*, s.v. *charge,* sense 13); if this is what the poet intended, the line becomes a statement of the desirability of freedom from the need to seek the protection of a higher authority.

101–02.   Cf. Whiting, S.657: "He is bound at a stake that may not do but as he is bidden."

103.   *crane:* Turner (pp. 96/97) refers to cranes breeding in the marshy areas of England in his own day.

106.   Cf. Tilley, W.423; Whiting, W.306: "let this wind over-blow."

107–10.   The exact meaning of the hawk's words is by no means certain. Lines 107–08 may be glossed: "whoever can blow to please (or satisfy) long necks (i.e., birds such as herons and cranes) gives great pleasure." The tone would appear to be ironic; *blowe* is used metaphorically, in response to the use of *ouerblowe* in the previous line, with the implied sense of "act." Thus, the hawk is countering the pacificism and fatalism of the heron and the crane (the view that it is better to wait inconspicuously for the things which threaten one's well-being to disappear) with a statement of aggressive individualism, to the effect that some people are capable of actually initiating events. The following two lines are similarly obscure, but their gist would appear to be that the common birds can have no peace since they must perpetually flee from danger. All texts read *meneth* in line 110, but since this makes extremely poor sense, and since this passage is concerned with the contrast between rest and movement, the minor emendation to *meueth* has been made. Lines 109–10 are tentatively glossed: "for the common birds who have no rest never move with the nobles"—i.e., have to flee wherever they can in order to avoid their enemies, and do not have the freedom of movement enjoyed by the more powerful birds.

112.  This view is, of course, in direct contrast to the pacificism advocated by the heron and the crane.

119.  The pairing of the robin and the wren may reflect the popular notion that these birds are the male and female of the same species. This idea is exemplified in the nursery rhyme, "The Marriage of Cock Robin and Jenny Wren" (text in Lack, pp. 15–20), and in the popular rhyme: "The robin redbreast and the wren / Are God Almighty's cock and hen" (Lack, p. 90; cf. *HB* 188–89 and note). It may also be suggested in the pairing of the two birds in *The Birds' Praise of Love,* 41–48.

127.  *comyn house:* See n.53, and Introduction, pp. 35–36.

129–30.  There are clearly two distinct versions of these lines, making the same statement, one through a positive construction (the hawk will destroy all birds), the other through a negative construction (the hawk will leave no bird alive).

131.  *For nere:* The reading *in* at the beginning of this line in WKV results from erroneous repetition of the beginning of the following line on the part of a scribe or compositor.

133.  *Theyr . . . plucketh:* Cf. Whiting, F.104: "to pull (pluck) one's feathers." See also *PB* n.304.

137–44.  An interesting parallel occurs in Dunbar, *Thistle,* 121–26, where one of the first duties required by Dame Nature of the newly-crowned eagle is that he should regulate the hunting of other birds by predators.

138.  *fordone:* The emendation makes for a more natural sense ("ruin, kill") than the textual reading *forgone* (possibly "overlook": *OED,* s.v. *forgo,* sense 2). In either case, the exigencies of the rhyme scheme have forced the poet to adopt an inappropriate past form in place of the infinitive.

142.  *a payre of gesse:* The singular form is often used with the plural sense (see *OED,* s.v. *jess*). A jess is a narrow strip of leather fastened to each of the hawk's legs—hence a *payre of gesse.* The swivel and leash are attached to the loose end of the jess; when the hawk is flown they are removed, but the jesses remain in place. Thus the wearing of jesses here signifies that the hawk is under the control of another. For further information on hawks' "furniture," see Hands, pp. 104–05.

145.   *Cornysshe dawe:* This name is commonly applied to the chough: see Hare, p. 146; Swainson, p. 74; and Swann, p. 60.

146.   Cf. Whiting, L.110: "Who will have law must have money"; Tilley, L.125: "A lawyer will not plead but for money."

148.   *Go bet . . . go:* lit., "go better, penny, go better, go,"—i.e., a man does better if he has money—probably a quotation from the refrain of "Sir Penny," a fifteenth-century poem (*IMEV,* no. 2747) found in MS. Sloane 2593 and printed in Wright, 1841 (II.A), p. 361. In full it reads, "Go bet, Peny, go bet, go, for thou mat makyn bothe frynd and fo." The poem argues that with money a man may purchase respect, companionship, and the protection of the law (cf. *PB* 146). There is perhaps a certain irony in assigning this comment to the *Cornysshe dawe,* since choughs had a reputation for thieving—to which reference is made, e.g., by Chaucer (*PF,* 345) and by Turner (pp. 90–93); see further, Rowland, p. 20.

150–52.   The chough was notorious as a chatterer, as reflected (e.g.) in *Hamlet,* V.ii.89, and *The Tempest,* II.i.257.

150.   Tilley, S.112; Whiting, S.77.

152.   Tilley, T.403; Whiting, T.384. Cf. Prov. 25:15.

153.   On the abrupt transition from the story of the hawk to that of the crow, see Introduction, pp. 33–34.
*rowe:* The emendation of *rewe* (W) to *rowe* (KLV) is justified by the rhyme. *Rew* is attested by the *OED,* and *by rew/row* ("in order, one after another") is listed under both words.

154.   *crowe:* For the crow's poor reputation in bird lore and literature (cf. next line), see Knortz, pp. 93–123; Robinson, 1883 (III.8), pp. 133–40; Rowland, pp. 35–38; Swainson, pp. 84–85; and Swann, pp. 41–42.

155.   Cf. Whiting, C.455: "Good counsel is good for him that will do after it."

159–60.   The crow's ability to predict rain is a commonplace of bird lore from the classical period on: see, e.g., Isidore, XII.vii.44; McCulloch, p. 108; Bartholomaeus, 12:10; Topsell, p. 222; and Swann, p. 42. Medieval and Renaissance writers on the subject usually include a reference to Virgil's observation in the *Georgics* (1:388–89); similar comments from Cicero and Lucretius are quoted by Martin (p. 69). The idea is also worked into certain stories about the crow: thus, in Chaucer's *Manciple's Tale,* part of the crow's punishment is that he must "evere crie agayn tempest and rayn" (Chaucer, *CT,* 9:301).

161.   *hyghwalle:* "green woodpecker." The name occurs as "hewhole, huhol" in Turner, who incidentally confirms the

identification of this bird as *picus viridis* (pp. 88/89, 114/15). For the varied forms in which this name appears, see *MED*, s.v. *hegh-wal;* Swainson, pp. 99–100; and Swann, pp. 110, 122. The emended text is based on L. The WKV reading *nyghtwhale,* which does not correspond to any known English bird name, probably results from scribal or editorial attempts to make sense of an unfamiliar word (perhaps influenced by such other names as "night-owl" and "nightingale"). Cf. *PB* n.177.

163. *with Iohan and Iacke:* i.e., with everybody.

164. Tilley, S.531; Whiting, S.378.

169. There seems no particular reason for associating these two birds with the observation in lines 170–72.

170. Whiting, G.347.

172. The sense appears to be: "who does not have to be responsible for (or support) others."

177–84. The poet now switches back briefly to the story of the hawk. See Introduction, pp. 33–34.

177. *specke:* "greater spotted woodpecker." This word is sometimes used loosely to signify simply "woodpecker," but in view of the presence of another kind of woodpecker in the poem (the *hyghwalle, PB* 161) it seems likely that the poet is using it specifically. Turner (pp. 148/49) identifies the "specht" or "wodspecht" as *dendrocopos major* and distinguishes clearly between it and the "hewhole" (green woodpecker). Cf. *PB* n.161.

182. Cf. the Bird's words of warning in Lydgate's *Churl:* "And whoo desireth to clymbe to hih a-loftt / Bi sodeyn torn, felith often his fal vnsoftt" (lines 209–10).

183–84. Tilley, C.357; Whiting, C.235.

185–254. The poet now resumes the story of the crow. See Introduction, pp. 33–34.

190. *poste:* "power, strength": see *OED*, s.v. *poustie, pousty.*

191. A typical formula for the introduction of a proverb.

192. Tilley, H.119; Whiting, H.62.

193. *tydyffre:* probably "titmouse." The *OED* is noncommittal, glossing "name of some small bird," while, at the other extreme, Swainson (p. 34) takes the word to signify the "blue tit" in particular. Newton, 1896 (III.B), p. 962; Swann (p. 243); and Hare (p. 176) consider it to be a general and unspecific word for "titmouse"—the most likely interpretation. The *OED* lists only the form *tidife (–ive);* the form with *–r* (as in WKV) is, however, attested by Newton—though the word occurs more commonly without the final *–r.*

196.   Tilley, B.363; Whiting, B.301.

200.   *the blynde . . . flye:* Tilley, B.451; Whiting, B.348. This proverb forms part of the refrain in the lyric, "Scorn of Women": Robbins, 1955 (II.A), pp. 224–25.

208.   *Knaue, knaue:* Used to typify words spoken by a bird which does not understand the meaning of what he says. It has some similarity to "Walk knaue, walke," the cry of the parrot in Lyly's *Midas,* I.ii.44—accorded proverbial status by Tilley (K.140).

211.   *fle:* see n.96.

213.   *semowe:* The usual form of this word is *semew(e),* but the rhyme suggests that the L reading is correct. The *OED* does not list *semow(e)* as a form, but it occurs in a brief piece of prose intended for educational purposes, contained in the fifteenth-century MS. Harley 1002, and printed in Wright, 1951 (II.B).

214.   The hawk's words provide an answer to the question asked in line 210.
*sory:* This could represent either *sorry* (in the sense "vile, wretched") or *sory* (ON *saurigr*) "filthy, dirty."

222.   A version of Tilley, P.424: "He that has plenty of goods shall have more, he that has but a little shall have less, and he that has right nought right nought shall possess." Cf. Whiting, N.145: "He that has nought shall always bide poor, etc. (*varied*)," and Matt. 13:12, 25:29; Luke 8:18, 19:26.

224.   Tilley, T.125.

226.   Tilley, G.354: "He may shoe the goose"; Whiting, G.389: "To shoe the goose" i.e., to waste one's time in fruitless or trivial activity. Medieval artists sometimes portrayed a blacksmith literally fixing horseshoes to the feet of a goose—as in the carving at Beverley Minster (illustrated in Wright, 1865 [III.B] p. 92), and the manuscript marginalia reproduced in Randall (plates 579 and 580).

229.   The intended sense would seem to be, "it is a matter agreeable to reason that all men should have such honor"—i.e., that no one should be a "knave."

231–32.   The hawk's point is that the cormorant is expressing the reverse of the truth.

233–34.   Though the cormorant in literature is often identified with negative qualities or experiences, these are usually associated directly with greed and consumption—as in Chaucer, *PF,* 362 and in Drayton, *Poly-Olbion,* song 25, line 127. See further, Rowland, pp. 30–31.

234.   Cf. Whiting, L.570: "Such as you love such are you like."

240.   Cf. Tilley, K.128: "A knave in grain"; K.133: "Once a knave and ever a knave."

241.   Whiting, T.94.

244–46.   There is an unintended irony in the hawk's words, since the orderly ruling of the community will necessitate that restraint should be imposed upon him.

247.   The saying, "to pluck a crow"—used, e.g., in Skelton, *SP,* line 396—alludes to this episode in the story of the crow's borrowed feathers.

249.   The feathers would, of course, have been a variety of colors, and *reed* is perhaps here used loosely to suggest "bright colors."

250.   *of the fyrste heed:* This phrase is used literally to describe "a deer, etc. at the age when the antlers are first developed," and hence metaphorically "a man newly ennobled or raised in rank" (*OED,* s.v. *head,* sense 6.b). Irony may be intended in applying the phrase to a character newly deprived of nobility and reduced in rank.

255–76.   The poet returns to the story of the hawk. See Introduction, pp. 33–34.

261.   *cheson:* The meaningless *theson* may have originated from scribal or editorial unfamiliarity with this word.

262.   *in truste is treason:* Tilley, T.549; Whiting, T.492.

264.   *hokes:* "talons." The meaning seems self-evident, despite the fact that this is not a sense acknowledged in the *OED,* s.v. *hook.* This usage should, perhaps, be regarded as an extension of *OED* sense 1.b, "a recurved and pointed organ or appendage of an animal or plant"—for which, however, the earliest citation is dated 1666.

273–75.   *Now . . . foo:* Whiting, N.179: "Now (this) now (that)."

274–75.   Although included on the authority of L alone, the content of these lines accords well with the proverbial tone of much of the poem; without them the present lines 273 and 276 would form a two-line stanza for which there is no parallel in the text.

276.   *Thus goeth the worlde:* Whiting, W.665.

277–92.   Having completed the story of the hawk, the poet goes on to conclude that of the crow. See Introduction, pp. 33–34.

285.   Since this would appear to be a further reference to the theme of the borrowed feathers, it is an odd inconsistency that

the "borrower" should be the raven and not the crow. See Introduction, pp. 33–34.

287.  *Nor:* WKV *for* was copied erroneously from the following line.

287–88.  Cf. the argument offered earlier by the *tydyffre* (*PB*, 193–96).

289.  *iaye:* There seems to be no particular significance in the attribution.

291–92.  Presumably because "the egle doth flye / Hyest in the skye" (Skelton, *PS*, 550–51).

292.  Cf. Tilley, F.164: "he would fain fly (flee) but he wants feathers."

293–312.  On this general moralizing conclusion, see Introduction, pp. 33–34.

293–96.  This stanza is entitled *Sapiencia* in KV.

293–94.  The point of the comparison is, presumably, that embers die just as feathers fade.

297–312.  This final section is entitled *Concludent* in KV.

297.  The ostrich's ability to consume metal objects is a commonplace of encyclopedias, bestiaries, and animal lore, probably derived from Pliny's statement (Pliny, *NH*, 10:1) that the ostrich can eat anything: see McCulloch, pp. 67–68; White, pp. 121–22; and Bartholomaeus, 12:34. (Apparently ostriches will eat small pieces of metal: see Tristram, 1877 [III.B], pp. 238–39.) There are many references to this notion in sixteenth-century literature, including Skelton's lines in *PS:* "The estryge, that will eate / An horshowe so great, / In the stede of meate, / Such fervent heat / His stomake doth freat" (478–82). An ostrich is depicted in the process of consuming a horseshoe in Bibliothèque Nationale (Paris) MS. latin 1076, f.16ᵛ (reproduced in Randall, plate 545).

299–300.  It might seem curious to find the swallow—which is so often celebrated for its speed and grace—associated with sloth; however, some writers on bird lore state that the swallow sleeps through the winter and reawakens in the spring (see, e.g., Turner, p. 149; and Swann, pp. 231–32). Cf. *HB* n.241.

301.  *trewe as turtyll:* Tilley, T.624: Whiting, T.542. See *HB* n.199.

303.  *glotonous gull:* This is not an adjective commonly associated with the gull in contemporary literature—though its application would, of course, be endorsed by observation.

304.  *his fethers pull:* Cf. Whiting, F.104: "To pull (pluck) one's feathers," and *PB* 133.

305. *as hasty as a wype:* Cf. Whiting, W.720: "As wroth as a wype." The meaning of *hasty* in this usage could be "precipitate," "precocious," or "speedy." Though the first of these is most appropriate in this particular context, the second offers a more familiar association for the lapwing *(wype):* cf. *Hamlet,* V.ii.181.

307. *fethers:* Perhaps with a punning second sense, "quills, pens."

# Glossary

## Note to the Glossary

THE GLOSSARY IS STRICTLY SELECTIVE, LISTING ONLY OB-
scure words and common words spelled unusually or
used in unfamiliar senses. All spellings of listed words are
recorded. In cases where a number of different spellings
occur, headwords are either composite or else represent
the commonest spelling. When words appear more than
once in either text, references to the first two instances are
given; if a word appears three or more times in either text,
the final reference is followed by "etc." Parts of speech are
specified only when necessary in order to differentiate be-
tween various usages. Normal inflected forms are not re-
corded separately.

| | |
|---|---|
| **aboute** | around, *PB* 143 |
| **abyde** | remain, dwell, *PB* 131 |
| **ado** | trouble, *PB* 82 |
| **aduysement** | deliberation, consultation, *PB* 209 |
| **agayne** | in reply, in response, *PB* 79 |
| **an** | on, *PB* 291 |
| **angelicall** | angel-like, *HB* 66 |
| **aray(e)** | attire, dress, *PB* 162, 176, etc. |
| **armony** | harmony, *HB* 24 |
| **astrych** | ostrich, *PB* 297 |
| **auaunt** | vaunt, boast, *PB* 228 |
| **auayle** | *v.* avail, afford help, *PB* 112; prosper, *PB* 114; *sb.* advantage, benefit, *PB* 286 |
| | |
| **bade** | announced, threatened, *PB* 43 |
| **bedene** | *see* **bydene** |

| | |
|---|---|
| **bere** | *b. hym lowe,* conduct himself humbly, *PB* 105; *b. out,* be responsible for, support, *PB* 172 |
| **best** | best people, nobles, *PB* 110 |
| **bet** | better, *PB* 148 |
| **blustred** | blasted, uttered a blasting sound, *PB* n.87. |
| **bottore** | bittern, *PB* n.87. |
| **brest** | voice in singing, *HB* n.64 |
| **briefe** | breve, short note in music, *HB* 101 |
| **by** | in consequence of, through *PB* 209; *b. rowe,* in order, one after another, *PB* n.153; *b. thy wyll,* with your consent, *PB* 149 |
| **bydene, bedene** | together, *PB* 205; immediately, *PB* 307 |
| **bylles** | beaks, *PB* n.7 |
| **byrdes** | young ones, nestlings, *HB* 212 |
| **can(ne)** | know, *PB* 21, 53; can do, *PB* 170 |
| **charge** | custody, responsibility for someone, *PB* n.98 |
| **cheson** | occasion, cause, *PB* 261 |
| **clerke** | scholar, *PB* 191 |
| **come** | *c. of,* be derived from, *PB* 240 |
| **comunes** | *see* **comyns** |
| **comynalte** | community, commonwealth, *PB* 246 |
| **comyn house** | House of Commons, *PB* n.127 |
| **comyns, comunes** | the common people, *PB* 53, 109, etc. |
| **conforte** | gladden, entertain, *HB* 8 |
| **Cornysshe dawe, Cornysshe** | chough, *PB* 145, 149 |
| **cote** | coot, *PB* 88 |
| **counseyll, cownselle** | judgement, prudence, *PB* 155, 158; advice, opinion, *PB* 160, 289; purpose, intention, *PB* 50 |
| **crafte** | skill, cunning, strength, *PB* 94 |
| **creked** | uttered a harsh cry, croaked, *PB* 95, 103 |
| **dawe** | *see* **Cornysshe dawe** |
| **debate** | strife, contention, *PB* 13 |
| **decayd** | decayed, impaired, *HB* n.64 |
| **degre** | estate, station in life, *PB* 182 |
| **dere** | harm, mischief, *PB* 89, 124 |
| **disporte** | relaxation, recreation, *HB* 7 |
| **distylde** | showered, sprinkled, *HB* 5 |
| **dobchyk** | dabchick, *PB* 88 |
| **domesticall** | domestic, *HB* 122 |
| **dou(u)e** | dove, *HB* 169; *PB* 63 |
| **dyssyuer** | dissolve, disperse, *PB* 278 |
| **ellamy** | e-la-mi, the singing of the note E, *HB* n.39 |
| **ese** | pleasure, *PB* 108 |

| | |
|---|---|
| **estate** | social group, class, *HB* 146, *PB* 14; order, *HB* 71; display of grandeur, *PB* 166 |
| **facyon** | fashion, manner, *HB* 226 |
| **faste** | *f. by,* close to, *PB* 102 |
| **fath** | faith, *HB* n.51 |
| **fayle** | lack, want, *PB* 51; become deficient in, *PB* 292 |
| **fayne** | gladly, willingly, *PB* 206 |
| **fle** | fly, *PB* n.96, 99, etc. |
| **fleteth** | glides away, vanishes, *PB* 74 |
| **flyght-rype** | fit to fly, *PB* 306 |
| **folde** | *see* **many a folde** |
| **foly** | ? wickedness, *PB* n.77 |
| **for** | on account of, *PB* 63 |
| **fordone** | ruin, kill, *PB* n.138 |
| **fresshe** | bright, finely-dressed, *PB* 174, 286 |
| **galaunt** | gorgeous, smart, *PB* 176 |
| **gesse** | jesses, *PB* n.142 |
| **glede** | ember, fire, *PB* 293 |
| **go** | *g. bet,* go better, go quicker, *PB* n.148; *g. by,* go unregarded, *PB* 28 |
| **good** | prosperity, well-being, *PB* 294 |
| **gretter** | *the g.,* with more distinction, prominence, *PB* 216 |
| **grype** | vulture, *PB* n.11 |
| **hande** | *vnder the h.,* under the charge, care, *PB* 271 |
| **hasty** | precipitate, precocious, *PB* n.305 |
| **heed** | *of the fyrste h.,* newly-made, *PB* n.250 |
| **herbor** | arbor, garden, *HB* 18 |
| **hokes** | talons, *PB* n.264 |
| **hold(e)** | *h. with,* maintain allegiance to, *HB* 135–36, 262 |
| **honeste** | decency, comeliness, *PB* 189 |
| **hyghwalle** | green woodpecker, *PB* n.161 |
| **ioly** | gallant, self-confident, *PB* 78 |
| **knaue** | one of low condition, *PB* 221; *k., k.,* meaningless statement, *PB* n.208 |
| **kynde** | *sb.,* kin, race, *PB* 139; nature, natural disposition, *PB* 301; *adj.,* natural, innate, *PB* 252 |
| **lafte** | left, finished, *PB* 93 |
| **leeff** | agreeable, *PB* 275 |
| **lesse** | lie, *PB* 157 |
| **lettyng** | hindrance, delay, *HB* 29 |

| | |
|---|---|
| **lewed** | ignorant, foolish, *PB* 68 |
| **loke** | inspect, examine, *PB* 307 |
| **long** | long note in music, *HB* 101 |
| **lose** | *adj.*, free, *PB* 96; *adv.*, free, *PB* 99 |
| **lot** | condition, portion in life, *PB* 63 |
| **loth** | unpleasant, *PB* 275 |
| **lusty** | pleasant, delightful, *HB* 6 |
| **lyght** | alight, descend, *HB* 19, 173 |
| | |
| **make** | mate, *PB* 101 |
| **many a folde** | many times, with many repetitions, *PB* 133 |
| **mauys** | song thrush, *HB* n.38 |
| **meane** | mean, middle part in a harmonized performance, *HB* 45 |
| **mende** | improve, rectify, *PB* 186 |
| **merely** | merrily, *HB* 82 |
| **mery** | pleasing, agreeable, *PB* 60, 64 |
| **mete** | suitable, fit, HB 236 |
| **mewe** | shut up, *PB* n.48, 52 |
| **morecocke** | red grouse, *PB* 79 |
| **myscheuous** | calamitous, harmful, *PB* 179 |
| **mysse** | injury, wrong, *PB* 155 |
| | |
| **nocke** | *out of n.*, out of order, *PB* n.80 |
| **noyse** | strife, contention, *PB* 5; outcry, clamor, *PB* 255 |
| | |
| **on** | in, consisting in, *HB* 101 |
| **oration** | prayer, *HB* 248 |
| **ordayne** | set up, establish, *PB* 3 |
| **osyll** | blackbird, *HB* 223; *PB* n.81 |
| **other** | others, *PB* 266 |
| **ouerblowe** | blow over, abate, *PB* 106 |
| **ought** | aught, anything whatever, *PB* 76, 175 |
| | |
| **page** | low person, knave, *PB* 250 |
| **part** | depart, *PB* 302 |
| **parte** | function, duty, *HB* 92 |
| **pelfe** | booty, pilfered property, *PB* 233 |
| **pen** | feather, *PB* 120 |
| **popyng(ei)ay** | parrot, *HB* n.25; *PB* 39 |
| **poste** | power, strength, *PB* n.190 |
| **postle** | apostle, messenger, *HB* 106 |
| **prating** | chattering, *PB* 27 |
| **pretend(e)** | intend, *HB* 321; *PB* 265 |
| **pricke** | set down (musical notes), *HB* n.223 |
| **prosperyte** | good fortune, success, *PB* 245 |
| **proue** | prove, demonstrate, *HB* 160, 170 |

| | |
|---|---|
| **pull** | pluck, pluck out, *PB* 304 |
| **purpose** | set forth, present, *HB* 267 |
| **put** | *p. all in*, entrust all to, commit all to, put all in the hands of, *PB* 268 |
| **pye** | magpie, *HB* 115; *PB* 27 |
| **pyke** | *hym . . . p.*, take himself off quickly, *PB* 254 |
| **quere** | choir, *HB* 293 |
| **ra** | row, *HB* 310 |
| **rayment** | clothes, apparel, *PB* 186 |
| **reason** | statement, *PB* 67; ground, cause, *PB* 135; *is r.*, is a matter agreeable to reason, *PB* n.229 |
| **redde** | agreed upon, resolved, *PB* 282 |
| **redrest** | arranged, put in order, *HB* 134 |
| **reformeth** | repairs, corrects, *PB* 155 |
| **reherse** | recite, say over, *HB* 69, 166, etc. |
| **rey** | the musical note "re," *HB* n.185 |
| **rombled** | rumbled, made a rumbling sound, *PB* 63 |
| **round** | mellow, *HB* n.41 |
| **routhe** | a matter for regret, *PB* 34 |
| **rule** | maxim, principle, *PB* 228 |
| **season** | *out of s.*, inappropriately, inopportunely, *PB* 38 |
| **semble** | assembly, gathering, *PB* 278 |
| **semowe** | seagull, *PB* n.213 |
| **sette** | resolved, *PB* 10; *s. by*, held in esteem, regard, *PB* 171 |
| **shent** | reproved, punished, *PB* 32 |
| **shewed** | *forth s.*, put forth, *PB* 67 |
| **sho** | *v.*, shoe; *s. the goos*, shoe the goose, i.e., engage in fruitless activity, *PB* n.226 |
| **skyll** | discrimination, judgement, *PB* 53; that which is reasonable, right, *PB* 269 |
| **sory** | vile, wretched, *or* filthy, dirty, *PB* n.214 |
| **sot** | sweet, *HB* n.71 |
| **sothe** | sooth, truth, *PB* 32, 36 |
| **sous, sowse** | plunge, immerse, *PB* n.90, 128 |
| **specke** | greater spotted woodpecker, *PB* n.177 |
| **spede** | prosper, thrive, *PB* 198 |
| **spring** | begin to appear, *HB* 9 |
| **states** | estates of the realm, *PB* 138 |
| **sterlynge** | starling, *PB* 31 |
| **stonde** | flourish, *PB* 130 |
| **syth** | since, seeing that, *HB* 175 |

| | |
|---|---|
| **take** | *t. me,* commit myself, *PB* 197; *t. his wyll,* do as he wishes, *PB* 18; *t. . . . the wrong,* suffer harm, injustice, *PB* 16 |
| **tente** | notice, heed, *PB* 210 |
| **terme** | expression, *PB* 163 |
| **than** | therefore, *HB* 117, 190 |
| **thycke** | abundant, plentiful, *HB* 224 |
| **tower** | lofty flight, soaring, *HB* n.261 |
| **tuned** | sang, *HB* 58 |
| **turtyll, tyrtle** | turtle dove, *HB* 199; *PB* 301 |
| **tydyffre** | titmouse, *PB* n.193 |
| | |
| **ut** | the musical note "do," *HB* n.185 |
| | |
| **verament** | truly, *PB* 31 |
| **vouchesaue** | grant, permit, *PB* 230 |
| | |
| **ware** | goods, *PB* 224 |
| **waterhenne** | moorhen, *PB* 88 |
| **well** | well-being, *PB* 276 |
| **weneth** | expects, anticipates, *PB* 46; thinks, supposes, *PB* 253 |
| **who** | whoever, *PB* 12, 45, etc. |
| **with, wyth** | among, *PB* 14, 17, etc.; by, *PB* 58 |
| **wode** | mad, *PB* 173 |
| **wolde** | wish, *PB* 178 |
| **worshyp** | honor, *PB* 229 |
| **wot(e)** | know, *HB* 62; *PB* 199 |
| **wreake** | harm, injury, *PB* 24 |
| **wunt** | wont, *HB* n.97 |
| **wype** | lapwing, *PB* 305 |
| **wyth** | *see* **with** |

# Index of Bird Names

NAMES ARE LISTED AS THEY ARE SPELLED IN THE texts. In cases of obscure or unfamiliar names or forms, cross-references are provided under the modern equivalents. All spellings of each name are listed. If one spelling occurs more frequently than the other, it is used as the headword. In cases where names occur more than once in either text, references to the first two occurrences are given. If the name occurs three or more times in either text, the final line-reference is followed by "etc." Names which occur in the texts only in their plural form are here represented by the equivalant singular. Inflected forms are not specified separately.

103

| | |
|---|---|
| greater spotted woodpecker | *see* **specke** |
| green woodpecker | *see* **hyghwalle** |
| grouse, red | *see* **morecocke** |
| grype | *PB* 11 |
| gull | *PB* 303; *see also* **semowe** |
| hawke, hauke | *HB* 259; *PB* 6, 24, etc. |
| heron | *PB* 103 |
| hyghwalle | *PB* 161 |
| iaye | *PB* 289 |
| lapwing | *see* **wype** |
| larke | *HB* 91; *PB* 111 |
| magpie | *see* **pye** |
| malarde | *PB* 95 |
| mauys | *HB* 38 |
| mistle thrush | *see* **thrusshe** |
| moorhen | *see* **waterhenne** |
| morecocke | *PB* 79 |
| nightyngale, nyghtyngale | *HB* 73; *PB* 55 |
| ostrich | *see* **astryche** |
| osyll | *HB* 223; *PB* 81 |
| parrot | *see* **popyngay** |
| partryge, pertryche | *HB* 49; *PB* 111 |
| pecocke, pecoke | *HB* 61; *PB* 169, 285 |
| pellycane | *HB* 211 |
| pheasant | *see* **fesaunt** |
| phenix | *HB* 157 |
| popyngay, popyngeiay | *HB* 25; *PB* 39 |
| pye | *HB* 115; *PB* 27 |
| quayle | *PB* 111 |
| rauyn | *PB* 285 |
| redbrest | *HB* 133; *see also* **robyn** |
| red grouse | *see* **morecocke** |
| robyn | *PB* 119; *see also* **redbrest** |
| sea gull | *see* **gull, semowe** |
| semowe | *PB* 213; *see also* **gull** |
| song thrush | *see* **mauys** |
| sparrowe | *HB* 265 |
| specke | *PB* 177 |
| sterlynge | *PB* 31 |
| swalowe | *HB* 235; *PB* 299 |
| swanne | *PB* 169, 296 |

# Appendices

## Appendix A

This text is based on the Breviary printed by Whytchurch, 1541 [vol. 1, ix^v–x ff.], collated with that of Petit, 1528 [vol. 1, ix^v–x ff.]. For full details, see Bibliography, Section IV.A. Abbreviations in the text have been expanded in the normal way. The single substantive variant is recorded below.

1  To deum laudamus: te dominum confitemur.
2  Te eternum patrem: omnis terra veneratur.
3  Tibi omnes angeli tibi celi et vniuerse potestates.
4  Tibi cherubin et seraphin incessabili voce proclamant.
5  Sanctus. Sanctus. Sanctus. Dominus deus sabaoth.
6  Pleni sunt celi et terra: maiestatis glorie tue.
7  Te gloriosus apostolorum chorus.
8  Te prophetarum laudabilis numerus.
9  Te martyrum candidatus laudat exercitus.
10  Te per orbem terrarum: sancta confitetur ecclesia.
11  Patrem: immense maiestatis.
12  Uenerandum tuum verum: et vnicum filium.
13  Sanctum quoque paracletum spiritum.
14  Tu rex: glorie christe.
15  Tu patris: sempiternus es filius.
16  Tu ad liberandum suscepturus hominem: non horruisti virginis vterum.
17  Tu deuicto mortis aculeo aperuisti credentibus regna celorum.
18  Tu ad dexteram dei sedes: in gloria patris.
19  Iudex crederis esse venturus.
20  Te ergo quesumus famulis tuis subueni: quos precioso sanguine redemisti.

21 Eterna fac: cum sanctis tuis in gloria numerari.
22 Saluum fac populum tuum domine: et benedic hereditati tue.
23 Et rege eos: et extolle illos vsque in eternum.
24 Per singulos dies benedicimus te.
25 Et laudamus nomen tuum in seculum: et in seculum seculi.
26 Dignare domine die isto: sine peccato nos custodire.
27 Miserere nostri domine: miserere nostri.
28 Fiat misericordia tua domine super nos: quemadmodum sperauimus in te.
29 In te domine speraui: non confundar ineternum.

---

25. seculi]   Petit seculii

## Appendix B

*TE DEUM:* ENGLISH TEXT

This text is based on the Marquess of Bute's translation of the Breviary [1:19–20]. For details, see Bibliography, Section IV. A.

1  We praise Thee, O God: we acknowledge Thee to be the Lord.

2  All the earth doth worship Thee, the Father everlasting.

3  To Thee all Angels cry aloud, the heavens, and all the Powers therein.

4  To Thee Cherubim and Seraphim continually do cry:

5  Holy, Holy, Holy Lord God of Sabaoth.

6  Heaven and earth are full of the majesty of Thy glory.

7  The glorious company of the Apostles praise Thee:

8  The goodly fellowship of the Prophets praise Thee:

9  The white-robed army of Martyrs praise Thee:

10  The holy Church throughout all the world doth acknowledge Thee:

11  The Father of an infinite Majesty:

12  Thine honorable, true and Only Son:

13  Also the Holy Ghost, the Comforter.

14  Thou art the King of glory, O Christ!

15  Thou art the everlasting Son of the Father.

16  When Thou tookest upon Thee to deliver man, Thou didst not abhor the Virgin's womb.

17  When Thou hadst overcome the sharpness of death, Thou didst open the kingdom of heaven to all believers:

18  Thou sittest at the right hand of God, in the glory of the Father:

19  We believe that Thou shalt come to be our Judge:
20  We therefore pray Thee, help Thy servants, whom
    Thou hast redeemed with Thy precious Blood.
21  Make them to be numbered with Thy Saints in glory
    everlasting.
22  O Lord, save Thy people, and bless Thine in-
    heritance.
23  Govern them, and lift them up for ever.
24  Day by day we magnify Thee;
25  And we worship Thy name, ever world without end.
26  Vouchsafe, O Lord, this day, to keep us without sin.
27  Have mercy upon us, O Lord, have mercy upon us.
28  O Lord, let Thy mercy lighten upon us, as our trust is
    in Thee.
29  O Lord, in Thee have I trusted: let me never be con-
    founded.

# The Renaissance English Text Society

The Renaissance English Text Society was founded to publish scarce literary texts, chiefly nondramatic, of the period 1475–1660. Originally during each subscription period two single volumes, or one double volume, were distributed to members, who may purchase previous publications, while supplies last, from Associated University Presses. Beginning in 1978, with the publication of Series IV, members are billed $15 annual dues regardless of whether there is a volume published during the year; all subscriptions are used for printing and publishing costs, and members will be credited with the amount they have paid toward each series when it appears.

Subscriptions should be sent to John Tedeschi at The Newberry Library, 60 West Walton Street, Chicago, Illinois 60610, USA. Institutional members are requested to provide, at the time of enrollment, any order numbers or other information required for their billing records; the Society cannot provide multiple invoices or other complex forms for their needs. Nonmembers may purchase copies of past publications still in print from Associated University Presses, 440 Forsgate Drive, Cranbury, New Jersey 08512, USA.

**FIRST SERIES**

Vol. I. *Merie Tales of the Mad Men of Gotam,* by A. B., edited by Stanley J. Kahrl, and *The History of Tom Thumbe,* by R. I., edited by Curt F. Buhler, 1965.

Vol. II. Thomas Watson's Latin *Amyntas,* edited by Walter F. Staton, Jr., and Abraham Fraunce's translation *The Lamentations of Amyntas,* edited by Franklin M. Dickey, 1967.

**SECOND SERIES**

Vol. III. *The dyaloge Called Funus,* a translation of Erasmus's colloquy (1534), and *A Very Pleasant and Fruitful Diologue called The Epicure,* Gerard's translation of Erasmus's colloquy (1545), edited by Robert R. Allen, 1969.

Vol. IV. *Leicester's Ghost,* by Thomas Rogers, edited by Franklin B. Williams, Jr., 1972.

**THIRD SERIES**

Vols. V–VI. *A Collection of Emblemes, Ancient and Moderne,* by George Wither, with introduction by Rosemary Freeman and bibliographical notes by Charles S. Hensley, 1975.

**FOURTH SERIES**

Vols. VII–VIII. *Tom a Lincolne,* by R. I., edited by Richard S. M. Hirsch, 1978.

**FIFTH SERIES**

Vol. IX. *Metrical Visions* by George Cavendish, edited by A. S. G. Edwards, 1980.

**SIXTH SERIES**

Vol. X. *Two Early Renaissance Bird Poems,* edited by Malcolm Andrew, 1984.